Sensei Secrets: Mentoring at Toyota Georgetown

A QUALITATIVE STUDY OF THE SENSEI-PROTÉGÉ RELATIONSHIP AT TOYOTA

A Dissertation
Submitted to the School of
Graduate Studies and Research
in Partial Fulfillment of the
Requirements for the Degree
Doctor of Philosophy

Steven R. Leuschel

Indiana University of Pennsylvania

August 2020

© 2020 Align Kaizen Publishing

All Rights Reserved

ISBN: 978-0-9991897-5-7

Title: Sensei Secrets: Mentoring at Toyota Georgetown: A Qualitative Study of the Sensei-Protégé Relationship at Toyota

Author: Steven R. Leuschel

Dissertation Chair: Dr. John A. Anderson
Dissertation Committee Members: Dr. Erin L. Conlin
Dr. Ramesh G. Soni

This study examines the developmental interactions between Japanese senseis (mentors) and early American leaders at Toyota Motor Manufacturing Kentucky (TMMK). More specifically, this study examines why and how these early American leaders transitioned from the initiation phase of a mentor relationship to the active and transformational participation of the cultivation phase. This research identifies characteristics of developmental interactions so that other leaders and mentors can effectively adapt Toyota-style management practices and thinking.

Though the professionalization of Toyota Production Systems (TPS), also known as *lean manufacturing*, or simply *lean*, has proven to be vast, the success rate of emulation and adaptation of sustained TPS has been low. One of the many problems that organizations face when adapting TPS is executive resistance and misunderstanding of lean management and leadership (Emiliani, 2018; Sherman, 1994). Toyota faced a similar problem of resistance when it hired leaders from other automotive companies into Toyota during the initial years at TMMK. Understanding how Toyota overcame this resistance offers insight into better mentoring for adapting TPS.

This study performs qualitative interviews using oral history and grounded theory techniques. It specifically identifies characteristics of the transition from the initiation to cultivation phases of mentor relationships within TMMK from 1986 to 1992. This research illustrates how leaders who never before experienced the Toyota culture experienced transformation within mentor relationships, which enabled them to adopt Toyota's frame of reference for solving problems and ultimately Toyota's culture. The findings may prove adaptable and beneficial for other leaders and executives adopting TPS.

ACKNOWLEDGMENTS

First and foremost, I would like to thank my wife, Mary, for her support during this process as well as my four children who came into this world during my Ph.D. journey: Edith, Henry, Augustine, and Gloria. My close mentors and advisors over the years that encouraged the Toyota Production System and its variations, including Rodger Lewis, Gary Quinlivan, David Adams, and Dr. Richard Kunkle. Without the work of the Kennametal Center for Operational Excellence and all those involved, my journey would not exist. To my advisors and professors at IUP, especially Dr. Valerie Gunter, Dr. John Anderson, Dr. Erin Conlin, and Dr. Ramish Soni, as well as my classmates in Cohort 16. Special thanks to Dr. Steven Phillips who helped with editing and input into the final version of this dissertation. Most importantly, I would like to thank all of those who participated in this research and those who will participate in future research.

Foreword

I met Steven in 2006 at a conference sponsored by the Kennametal Center for Operational Excellence. We had just published *The Toyota Way Fieldbook* (Liker & Meler, 2005), and I was doing several speaking engagements related to the material in the book. At the time Steven was an undergraduate at St. Vincent's College in Latrobe, Pennsylvania, and was doing course work related to the Toyota Production System (TPS or Lean Manufacturing). We had several good conversations, and Steven seemed genuinely interested in understanding the philosophical and cultural "secrets" behind Toyota's famed system.

We kept in touch over the years, and a few years ago Steven contacted me regarding his dissertation. He wanted to study and understand the mentoring process that occurred between the Japanese sensei's and the American workers during the early days at the Toyota plant in Georgetown, Kentucky (Toyota Motor Manufacturing Kentucky or TMMK). I was hired in July of 1987 in the first group of people who would supervise shop floor employees, and I was intrigued by his idea and agreed to be interviewed.

The process of learning at TMMK was both very demanding and frustrating. If you watched the *Kung Fu* television series or *The Karate Kid* movie you saw the student in both cases often being confused on the purpose of the lesson or whether the lesson was learned—snatch the pebble from my hand. The experience of learning from Toyota's masters was ten times as frustrating! I liken it to Navy Seal training. If you survived the experience you were a much better person at the end. Many did not survive and left early.

I did not understand the purpose of some of the lessons until many years later and still have occasional "ah-ha" moments related to things that happened over 30 years ago at Toyota. One example is depicted in the diagram below. On the first day of work at Toyota the mantra "You learn by doing" is repeated over-and-over. It seemed to me that Toyota was famous for achieving great results in their operations, and I thought the main point was to get results (doing). We put in incredible amounts of effort to create huge gains, but during the reviews by our Toyota mentors all we heard as feedback was a lot of questions. Questions that made it seem that they were not satisfied with the result.

For a number of years, I felt that there was no way to make the Toyota mentors happy. It did not matter what the result was, they always had questions and did not seem satisfied. I had my epiphany just after completing the *Fieldbook* a full decade after leaving Toyota. The operative word in the statement was *learn*, not *doing*. The questions that were asked were not due to dissatisfaction with the outcome. The questions were meant to determine the *process* of thinking. The mentors were training us to use a thinking process. It is easy to see the outcome of someone's efforts, but in order to understand the thinking process it is necessary to ask questions such as "What led you to that conclusion?" "How did you make that decision?" "What was it based on?"

It then occurred to me that at some point the student

had learned the lesson to a level where they no longer need regular mentoring—snatch the pebble! I refer to it as "self-learning." This kind of learning will continue as you apply the lessons over and over in different situations. Ultimately the goal was for the student to become a teacher who will develop "the next generation"—the term "mentors" was used, as well as the mantra "pass on your knowledge."

It also occurred to me that *real* learning begins when you start to teach others the lessons. As a consultant for over 20 years, I have adopted the methods used by the Toyota mentors. One key modification in my method is I try to make the students understand the difference between satisfied and happy. We can be happy with the results achieved, but we can never be satisfied—settled with—them. That goes against the philosophy of continuous improvement.

In my model I realized that some people get stuck in the first loop of "Learn by Doing" and always need direction from the mentor to know what to do. I believe that many times this is due to a desire to achieve what has been asked—a "just tell me what you want, and I will do it" mind set. We have all been conditioned through school to believe that for any question there is a right answer and a wrong answer. We want to get the right answer and succeed. The thinking process is not certain. The answer to most questions is "it depends." The fact is there is no *right* or *wrong* answer in the thinking process. There are only choices.

Steven has done an excellent job in this book of categorizing the key characteristics and behaviors of Toyota's mentors. Learning from these mentors was significantly different from learning in the traditional manner where all questions have correct and incorrect answers. In the thinking process there are choices and options, and all have trade-offs. There is no ideal condition. Mentors must provide direction without giving the solution. Mentors must pose questions without alluding to the answer—in legal terms, a leading question intended to elicit a certain response. Being a mentor requires patience. If the goal is to learn by doing the mentor must allow "failure" at times—Toyota taught that the only failure in the thinking process was a failure to learn a lesson.

Being an effective mentor is difficult. Somehow Toyota has managed to develop hundreds or thousands of effective mentors who did pass along their ability to future generations. Steven has identified the key behaviors and compiled stories from several of the TMMK mentees. In these stories you will see the common threads even though each of the TMMK employees had different mentors. When I hear stories of other mentees I am amazed at the similarities of our experience even though we worked in completely different parts of the plant. This book will help you learn the essence of effective mentoring from the hard work that Steven has done to bring the information to bear.

David Meier
Owner | Glenns Creek Distillery
President | Lean Associates, Inc
Co-Author *The Toyota Way Fieldbook* and *Toyota Talent*

Foreword

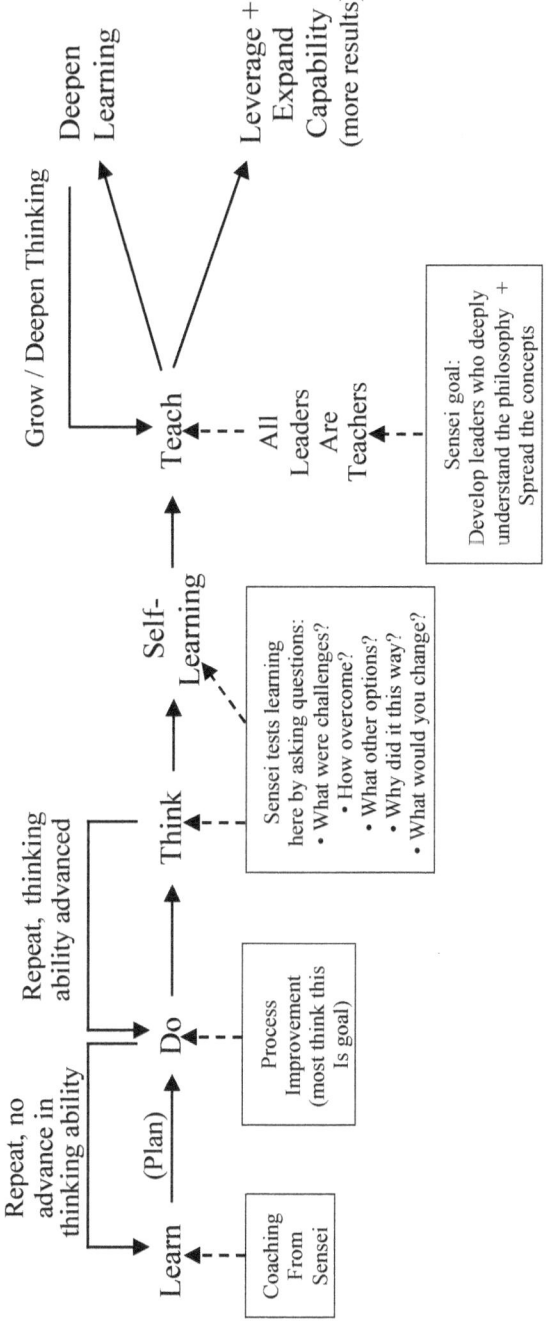

Preface

As David discussed in the Foreword, being a sensei involves questioning to grasp an understanding of a protégé's thinking. The emphasis is on LEARN in learn by doing. Similarly, I discuss in this book the sensei's questioning to understand the thinking of the protégé until the ability to self-learn is finally achieved.

Throughout the book, which is based on my PhD dissertation, I discuss the theory behind the *Process to Self-Learning with a Sensei* model, so readers can understand each part. The model shown in Figure X includes the phases of mentorship, the theme of protection, and the steps to self-learning. The process of mentorship, as we shall see, is driven by Scientific Management and Quality Management, both of which I discuss in detail as they apply to understanding the mentor relationships at Toyota Georgetown.

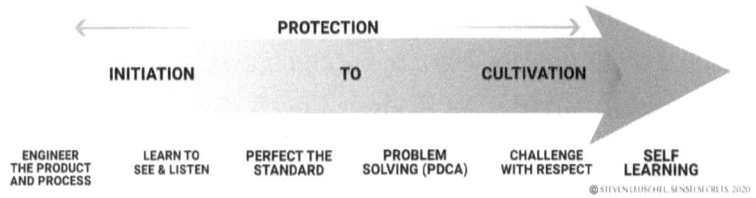

The phases of mentorship, discussed in this book, include: Initiation, Cultivation, Separation, and Redefinition. The model above focuses on the first two phases of mentor relationships: Initiation and Cultivation.

Sensei protected individuals from negative emotions, negative consequences, and negative interactions, especially during stressful times. Thus, protection—a sensei protecting a protégé—is a theme across the entire model and the two phases of Initiation and Cultivation. This protection was critically important during the emotionally stressful phases of the mentor relationship.

The full model also includes Scientific and Quality Management, both of which I discuss in detail as they apply to understanding the mentor relationships at Toyota Georgetown.

I arrived at this model through my dissertation research on my personal journey to achieve my PhD in Administration and Leadership Studies at Indiana University of Pennsylvania. Participants I interviewed for the dissertation included Rodger Lewis, Russ Scaffede, Catesby Prewitt, David Meier, Bob Wilson, and Jeff Merriss. I asked these participants a number of questions about their time during the early days of Toyota Georgetown, Toyota's first large scale fully owned plant in the U.S., to ultimately arrive at this model.

The first steps of the Initiation phase are: *engineering the product or process, learn to see and listen, perfect the standard,* and *problem solving*. As Rodger Lewis discusses, *engineering the product and process* is unique to Toyota as a way of achieving the standard without changing the actual engineering of the vehicle. Secondly, nearly every person I interviewed noted how their sensei helped them learn to see and listen. As David and others discuss, learning to see and learning to listen was one of the first tasks given to the protégés by their Japanese mentors—often described as standing on the X or standing in the circle.

When protégés *perfected the standard*, as John Allen says, then and only then are they going to be asked to solve problems and make improvements, but always under the guidance of a mentor. This step is critical for the protégé to demonstrate the ability to solve problems using a problem-solving methodology, thus the step is called *problem solving (PDCA or Plan-Do-Check-Act)* and takes place between the *Initiation* and *Cultivation* phases. Interactions between the sensei and protégé increase and the protégé, if applying the problem-solving methodology correctly, can begin to solve other problems by improving their thinking.

In the *Cultivation* phase, the sensei then *challenges with respect* but continues to ask questions to understand the protégé's thinking process. Once the protégé learns to ask their own questions, perform their own reflections, and solve problems more frequently on their own, they have in a large part advanced to *self-learning*, the final step in the *Cultivation* phase. Once this skill has been mastered, the relationship between the protégé and sensei becomes one of a colleague rather than a mentor.

This book will present both theory and history, including a brief history of Toyota and the theories of developmental relationships, scientific management, and quality management, among others, which I used to arrive at the model discussed here. Seven participants were interviewed from Toyota's earlier days at Toyota Georgetown. The themes that developed from the seven interviews are used throughout the book to describe the model as it emerged from the experiences of the participants during those early days.

I hope that readers are able to learn from this new model when establishing processes to develop people for improvement. Also, I hope readers enjoy the sometimes stressful, sometimes comical, but always informational stories found throughout this book.

Steven Leuschel

Contents

Chapter	Page

1 INTRODUCTION.. 25

    Background... 27
    Statement of the Problem 31
    Purpose Statement and Research Questions.......................... 32
    Research Design.. 33
    Significance of the Study.. 35
    Definition of Terms 35
    Assumptions, Limitations, and Delimitations 38
    Summary... 39

2 LITERATURE REVIEW 41

    Historical Context... 41
    United States Automobile Industry....................................... 42
        From Craft to Mass Production 42
        The U.S. Production System 44
        The Role of the Automobile in the U.S. Society and
            Economy 48
        The Challenges of the 1970s 48
    Toyota Motor Company.. 49
        Toyota Production System 50
            Toyota Manufacturing Comes to the United
                States 52
    The Diffusion of TPS in the United States............................ 58
        Toyota Supplier Support Center................................ 59
        Academia Promotes Kaizen 61
        Professionalization: Experts and
            Consultants.. 62
        Healthcare 63
    Organizational Theory and Change 65
        Scientific Management.. 66

Chapter	Page
Quality Management Theory	68
Leadership in Organizations	73
Leadership at Toyota	74
Mentoring: A Developmental Interaction	77
Types of Developmental Interactions	79
Mentoring	80
Mentoring and Coaching	82
Action Learning and Mentoring	82
Traditional Mentoring	83
Formal and Informal Mentoring	85
Characteristics of Mentoring	85
Phases of Mentoring	90
Initiation Phase	92
Cultivation Phase	92
Separation Phase	92
Redefinition Phase	93
Organizational Benefits of Mentoring	93
Mentoring in Japanese Culture	94
Summary	96
3 METHODOLOGY	99
Qualitative Research Methods	99
Case Study Techniques	100
Oral History Techniques	100
Grounded Theory Techniques	101
Narrative Analysis Techniques	102
Research Design	102
Research Questions	103
The Interview Process	104
Obtaining Accurate Oral History	104
Participants and Sampling	105
Setting	107
Instruments	107
Informed Consent and Final Release	108
Data Analysis	108
Sensei-Protégé Characteristics	109

Chapter	Page
Demographic and Other Characteristics	110
Emotional Behaviors and Negative Experiences	111
From Initiation to Cultivation	112
Mentoring Perspective	114
Considerations	114
Ethical Risks	115
Credibility and Trustworthiness	115
Confidentiality, Anonymity, and Privacy	116
Summary	116
4　RESULTS	118
Study Participants	119
Early Mandatory Developmental Relationships	121
Organizational Structure and Participant Roles	122
Characteristics of the Mentor Relationships at Toyota	126
Age and Gender of Participants	126
Perception of Knowledge/Experience	127
Duration, Purpose, and Timeframe	127
Schedule of Interactions, Organizational Distance, Direction, and Span	128
Location	129
Structure, Initiation, and Matching	129
Developmental Coordinator, Support, and Preparation	130
Trustworthiness of Senseis and Toyota	130
Separation and Redefinition	130
Summary of Early Mandatory Developmental Relationships	131
Mentoring and Protection	132
Stories of Protection	133
Story Number One: Americans Experience Frustration	134
Story Number Two: American Leader Protecting the Workforce	134

Chapter	Page
Story Number Three: Frustration of American Worker	136
Story Number Four: Mentee Stopped Production	137
Story Number Five: Protection from Inadvertent Neglect of Team Members	137
Story Number Six: Introduction of Total Preventative Maintenance (TPM)	138
Story Number Seven: Participant Experienced Negative Japanese Emotion	139
Story Number Eight: Come With What You Have	140
Story Number Nine: Protection From Negative Consequences of Failure	141
Summary of Emotionally Charged Stories	143
The Mentoring Process	147
Initiation and Scientific Management	148
Learning to See and Listen	149
Standing in the Circle	151
Perfect the Standard	158
Initiation Summary	160
Cultivation	160
Problem Solving	161
Challenging	165
Self-Learning	168
Turning Points to Cultivation	177
Cultivating Quality Management	179
Summary	180
5　DISCUSSION	183
Research Questions	184
The Path to Self-Learning	185
Characteristics of the Sensei Relationship	187
The Theme of Protection	190
Scientific Management Application and Quality Management Learning	194

Chapter	Page
Engineer the Product and Process	194
The Continual Search for Quality	197
Transformational Learning	199
Limitations and Future Research	204
Summary	205
The House of TPS	208
REFERENCES	214
APPENDICES	225
Appendix D – Toyota Oral History-Style Questions	225
Appendix E – Sensei Characteristics	227
Turning Points for Cultivation	232
Appendix F – Semi-Structured Interview Questions Regarding Mentors	234

LIST OF TABLES

Table		Page
1	General Motors Framingham Assembly Plant versus Toyota Takaoka Assembly Plant, 1986	52
2	Categories of Developmental Interactions	80
3	Career and Psychosocial Functions	84
4	Categories, Attributes, and Specific Characteristics of the Mentor-Protégé Relationships	86
5	Negative Mentoring Experiences, Categories, and Examples	89
6	Phases, Turning Points, and Characteristics of Mentoring Relationships	91
7	Names, Roles, and Interview Dates of Participants	106
8	Data Analysis Methods	109
9	Key Words for Separating Experience	113
10	Characteristics of Early Mandatory Relationships	131
11	Emotional Experiences	144
12	Mentoring Characteristics	188
13	Turning Points to Quality Management	204

LIST OF FIGURES

Figure		Page
1	United Auto Workers Strikes 1946–1979	46
2	General Motors and Toyota Learning at and From NUMMI	53
3	Transferring Knowledge of TPS From Japanese Sensei to Early U.S. Leaders at TMMK	59
4	Types of Developmental Interactions	79
5	Transition to Cultivation: TMMK 1986–1992	103
6	Structure of Formal Mentoring at Toyota	120
7	Structure of Informal Mentoring at Toyota	121
8	Formal Mentoring at Toyota's Suppliers	121
9	Reporting and Mentoring Relationships at TMMK	125
10	The Process From Initiation to Cultivation at Toyota	148
11	Path of Self-Learning Quality Management Model	186
12	Engineer the Standard and Develop Standards	195
13	Full Self-Learning Quality Management Model	198

CHAPTER ONE
INTRODUCTION

The Arab oil embargo and the ensuing oil crisis of 1973 had major consequences on the global automobile market. In the U.S., the oil embargo (1973-1974) drew attention to foreign automobiles, resulting in Japanese and other economical imports increasing nearly three percent in market share (Treece, 2013). This was in part due to the higher quality of small fuel-efficient imports compared to "hasty, ill-planned and poorly executed attempts" into making small cars by the U.S. auto-industry, particularly Ford and General Motors (Treece, 2013, p. 1). These factors influenced Toyota's motivation to establish its own manufacturing operation of small cars within the United States beginning with its 1974 purchase of the operations now known as Toyota Auto Body California, Inc. (TABC). The primary operation at TABC essentially completed the final assembly of trucks and truck beds for shipping within the United States. Toyota's foothold in the United States expanded in 1983 when the company undertook a joint venture with General Motors (GM) under the name of New United Motor Manufacturing, Inc. (NUMMI) at a recently closed GM plant in Freemont, California. For GM, the joint venture provided an opportunity to learn about Japanese systems of management and especially the highly regarded, highly profitable

Toyota Production System (TPS). For Toyota, NUMMI provided an opportunity to learn about working with an American workforce. Within two years, both of these companies would take the knowledge they learned from NUMMI and use that knowledge in new plants of their own.

Toyota's new plant was located in Georgetown, Kentucky, with construction starting in 1985. This plant would come to be called Toyota Motor Manufacturing Kentucky (TMMK). From the start, Toyota's approach at TMMK was to use experienced Japanese leaders, or senseis, from Toyota to mentor the newly hired American workforce to adopt TPS. The plant was initially greeted with controversy from community residents, but within three years that had largely dissipated. Currently, TMMK is the largest automobile plant worldwide and continues to operate with a unique blend of Japanese and Western management.

The experience of TMMK stands in stark contrast to the attempt by General Motors to keep and capture market share through the development of an enlightened Toyota-type workforce; most notably at GM's failed Saturn plant in Tennessee. Construction on the Spring Hill, Tennessee, plant started in 1985. At that time the Saturn plant was the largest one-time economic investment in U.S. history, as GM spent $5 billion constructing the plant (Sherman, 1994). While the Saturn company and brand were initially successful—by 1992 Saturn was awarded the highest possible rating for mechanical reliability by *Consumer Reports* (Sherman, 1994)—by 2010 GM had discontinued the franchise. Other U.S. organizations, many outside the automobile industry and even outside manufacturing, attempted to replicate both Japanese quality and Toyota-like production systems, hoping for better quality and higher profits (Cameron & Quinn, 2011). Though attempting to replicate these systems brought much success, arguably many of the successes were isolated or not sustained compared to Toyota's.

The success of TMMK demonstrates the possibility to successfully integrate TPS into U.S. firms; the failure of Saturn and other companies demonstrates that doing so is not easy. Unraveling the reasons behind the successes and failures of integrating Japanese management systems into U.S. operations is of pressing importance for those wanting to reproduce the TMMK experience in other U.S. companies. The present study adds one vital piece to this broader task, that of documenting the nature of the mentorship relationships established in TMMK during its formative years. Understanding the mentor or sensei role in adapting and transplanting TPS, especially during the early years of Toyota's plant in Georgetown, may provide insight into better ways to more successfully adapt TPS elsewhere. As Gary Convis, the first U.S. president at TMMK, stated: "We began to understand after a number of years that we had benefited from some inspired leadership in those early years. It makes you realize how important this all was to Toyota" (Chappell, 2007, p. 102). This study will explore those early relationships at TMMK, identify the characteristics of Toyota's approach at this facility, and draw lessons that might apply in other organizational contexts.

Background

Japan was the first non-Western country to industrialize and did so with its own unique trajectory. Ethnically, Japan is quite homogeneous, and it moved into the modern era with a culture that is far more collectivist in orientation and traditional in outlook than found in Western societies. In Japan, groups and family-type personal relationships are highly valued. Elders are respected but also expected to reciprocate the higher levels of prestige and authority afforded them by taking responsibility to help and protect younger individuals (Bright, 2005). These cultural imperatives extend into Japanese firms, where they shape a paternalistic relationship between management and workers and foster an environment of cooperation and trust (Ouchi, 1981).

Toyota Motor Corporation was founded in Japan in 1935, about 50 years after the first gasoline automobile was produced in Germany. Toyota would develop its unique approach to car manufacturing, which would become known as the Toyota Production System (TPS). Though influenced by what would become known as Japanese Management, shaped by the cultural imperative identified above, TPS is not synonymous with but rather constitutes a unique variant of Japanese Management.

The Toyota Production System was a creation of leaders during Toyota's early years. These include leaders such as Eija Toyoda and Taiichi Ohno, who took the innovations of automobile industry leaders such as Henry Ford, who created the mass moving assembly line, and Edward Budd, who developed unibody vehicle construction, and combined these innovations with the Japanese Management system and then added the modification of what is now referred to as lean production. It is the combination of these three elements that constitute the Toyota Production System (Aoki, 2015; Holweg, 2007).

Toyota's adaptation of lean production was an outgrowth of economic necessity. When it was founded in 1935, Toyota did not have the high capital investment needed for the economies of scale characteristic of the high-volume mass production made possible by the Ford-Budd approach. Therefore, Toyota closely aligned with the methodologies of craft production until the 1950s.

In the 1950s, Taiichi Ohno, a Toyota executive who had risen in the ranks from his original position as a shop supervisor, visited the United States to better understand companies like Ford. With its lack of capital investment, Toyota adapted the Budd-Ford approach to include minimal inventory as a way of increasing the company's cash position (Aoki, 2015; Holweg, 2007). Japanese management, which was characterized by highly productive industrial workgroups, largely influenced the human relations side of the Toyota Production System.

The business and academic worlds began to take note of the Toyota Production System in 1965 when the concepts of *Kanban*, an element of just-in-time inventory, were introduced to Toyota's suppliers (Holweg, 2007). Since the 1980s, Toyota and the Toyota Production System have received extravagant praise from academics and the Western business world; much of American manufacturing and healthcare has become known as lean manufacturing or simply lean (Fujimoto, 1999; IHI, 2005).

Scientific management and Total Quality Control theories had significant influence on TPS. Frederick W. Taylor's scientific management theory of the early 1900s states that to increase output, organizations should systemize work processes. This systemization is done by "dividing work into narrowly defined tasks, determining the 'one best way' to perform each task, train workers in the 'one best way,' measure their performance, and offering economic incentives for surpassing daily production quotas" (Tompkins, 2005, p. 67). Quality management theory built upon scientific management with Walter Shewhart's concept of statistical process control. Taylor's scientific management with Edward Deming and Joseph Juran's total quality management influenced the Japanese and in particular, Toyota. Preventing quality errors, as opposed to inspection and correction, is more logical and cost-effective, resulting in higher quality, lower inventory, and improved cash flow (Tompkins, 2005).

Though attempts to emulate TPS and other re-engineering initiatives have been widespread, the success rate of these attempts remains low (Cameron & Quinn, 2011). Many companies started a lean journey by restructuring work and changing processes to emulate the success of Toyota. This focus on only one element of TPS—restricting work into a lean format—while ignoring another vital elements of TPS—a culture of mutual trust and respect between employees, management, and the community—provides a likely explanation as to why so many efforts to integrate TPS into American firms has failed. As one leader, Kaplan, who studied and implemented aspects of TPS said, "transformation requires using lean as part of a comprehensive management system in concert with institutional culture change and new leadership approaches…" (Kaplan et al., 2014, p. 927). There was apparently something special in the early years of TMMK that helped lead to its sustained success, and this research attempts to uncover this important component of success by focusing on Toyota's developmental interactions during those years.

Statement of the Problem

"Mentor" has evolved into a term that means a wise and trusted teacher (Finley et al., 2007; Klauss, 1981; Marrelli, 2004). Similarly, sensei is a Japanese term meaning "respected teacher" and is characteristic of developmental relationships found in the martial arts and teaching at its best. Mentor-protégé relationships generally follow four phases: *initiation, cultivation, separation,* and *redefinition* (Bullis & Bach, 1989; Kram, 1983). I will use these phases of mentoring, specifically the initiation and cultivation phases, to guide my exploration into the characteristics of the sensei-protégé relationship and the nature of mentoring between Japanese and American employees during the early years of Toyota in Kentucky (Coghlan & Brydon-Miller, 2014; D'Abate et al., 2003; Riggs, 2015).

Many of the organizations that have attempted to implement TPS in the United States have not been successful in terms of sustained results. There is good reason to suspect these failures stem from an almost exclusive focus on one aspect of TPS—restructuring processes to implement lean production—while ignoring the Japanese management side of TPS. In other words, U.S. firms have not invested the time and hard work needed to implement a culture of cooperation and trust between workers and management. The sensei or mentorship relationship is a key mechanism by which such an organizational culture is transmitted and reproduced. Given the general lack of attention to cultural components in Japanese management by U.S. companies attempting to appropriate TPS, incorporating mentor relationships may also be a missing element of adapting

Japanese management. It remains instructive to note that organizational establishment and the fostering of such relationships *did* occur in one of the most successful and longest lasting production endeavors, Toyota Motors Manufacturing Kentucky. TMMK has not only operated for over 30 years; it presently exists as the largest automobile manufacturing plant in the world.

Purpose Statement and Research Questions

This study explores the developmental interactions between Japanese senseis and early American leaders at TMMK. The purpose of this study is to understand the characteristics of these interactions and to follow the development of these relationships through the four phases of initiation, cultivation, separation, and redefinition (Bullis & Bach, 1989; Kram, 1983). This research aims to identify crucial mentor-mentee interactions as they relate to TPS in the hope that leaders in other organizations can adapt Toyota-style production, leadership, and management systems. In this study I will address the following two research questions:

Research Question One. What are the characteristics of the developmental relationship between early leaders at TMMK and their Japanese counterparts? This research question aims to identify the most prominent relationship characteristics, including demographics, behaviors within the relationship, perceptions of knowledge, schedule of interactions, positive/negative experiences, and degrees of trust (D'Abate et al., 2003).

Research Question Two. What are common steps within the Japanese-American mentor relationship as perceived by American leaders transitioning from the initiation phase to the cultivation phase? Kram (1983) identifies the phases of a mentor relationship as initiation, cultivation, separation, and redefinition. This research question specifically aims to identify common actions senseis took to advance mentor-like relationships from the initiation phase to the cultivation phase of the relationship.

Research Design

I based this research on oral histories from a sample of participants that included former Toyota employees who worked at the Georgetown Toyota plant (which grew into TMMK) between 1986-1992 and those who surrounded them. Therefore, I focused on the case study of Toyota starting the Toyota Georgetown plant. I conducted interviews with these seven Americans, all former employees of Toyota in positions ranging from Team Leaders (a frontline supervisor) to General Managers and Vice Presidents. A handful of individuals were hired to the highest levels of leadership at Toyota, of which I interviewed three. The first group of midlevel managers consisted of a group of 26 group leaders, which I've referred to as the Group of 26, of which I interviewed two. Generally, these individuals had formal mentor-protégé relationships. Other participants included team members that had informal mentor-protégé relationships.

The methods I used in this study were designed to obtain a focused oral history elicited through semi-structured interviews. Following Valerie Yow's method (2014), I encouraged participants to bring historical documents to the interviews to triangulate and essentially verify stories. I then analyzed, using techniques borrowed from narrative analysis and grounded theory, interview transcriptions and supporting documentation such as materials from Toyota, written documents from the interviewees, photographs, and other documents provided by study participants. Specifically, I extracted stories using key words to determine the characteristics of those mentor-mentee relationships. With the data analysis, I aimed to answer the research questions via documenting the nature and characteristics of the mentor relationships and the turning points from initiation to cultivation in those relationships. In particular, I focused on identifying the actions that helped move protégés from the initiation phase to the cultivation phase during their time at Toyota.

I utilized grounded theory techniques by establishing categories based on key words. I then categorized stories of the sensei relationship by either initiation or cultivation phases based on key words relating to each phase. Once all the data were coded, I analyzed results to determine the characteristics and phases of the mentor-protégé relationship. I coded verbs associated with turning points and further analyzed and categorized them into initiation—interactions around work tasks—and cultivation—transformational and meaningful interactions (Glaser & Strauss, 2017; Merriam & Tisdell, 2016). Credibility and trustworthiness were addressed through narrative analysis.

Significance of the Study

This study is significant because the relationship between Toyota's Japanese mentors and American leaders may never be replicated on this scale again. This research explores the Japanese senseis' relationship with the early American leaders at Georgetown, a unique moment in time and place. Additionally, this study characterizes the process of transformation from the initiation phase to the cultivation phase of a mentor relationship in the TPS, thereby shedding light on the complexity of the transformation process. This research will provide a framework for future researchers to understand the mentor relationship transition. Having insight into the mentorship process provides insight into how organizations might use mentoring to drive organizational change leading to increased effectiveness, efficiency, and competitiveness.

Definition of Terms

Several terms will be used throughout this research that may have different meanings in different contexts. Below I present these terms and offer explanations addressing their use in this study.

Case Study Techniques. Case studies are generally characterized by efforts to document and explain events and processes in a bounded system, in this case, the Toyota organization, specifically TMMK from 1986-1992 (Merriam & Tisdell, 2016).

Developmental Interactions. These actions between, generally, two people at or around the workplace include coaching, apprenticeship, action learning, and tutoring. Based on the description of mentoring and Toyota's early senseis discussed in the literature, the relationships at TMMK seem to be mentoring relationships, but all developmental interactions will be discussed.

Early Toyota American Leader. A leader within Toyota hired between 1986 and 1992 to Toyota Motor Manufacturing Kentucky (TMMK) who was at a level higher than a frontline team leader.

Grounded Theory Techniques. Methods of grounded theory, such as aiming to find facts to be used to create a theoretical framework grounded in those facts (Merriam & Tisdell, 2016). This research does not claim to be grounded theory but rather utilizes some of its techniques.

Group of 26. The 26 initial U.S. group leaders that visited Toyota in Japan.

Japanese Management. Japan is a homogeneous collectivist culture characterized by family-type personal relationships with high respect for elders in which elders protect younger individuals. Translated into business management, many firms have paternalistic relationships between management and workforce, further resulting in cooperation and trust in the workplace (Bright, 2005; Ouchi, 1981).

Lean. One may argue that lean is the more academic or generic description of the specific Toyota Production System. However, throughout this dissertation, lean will be used almost synonymously with TPS to describe the adaptation of TPS.

Narrative Analysis Techniques. The technique of utilizing and interpreting oral history stories, including their structure, elements, and functions (Allen, 2017).

Oral History Techniques. This study deals with data from decades ago, so oral history techniques were utilized to capture the data and related stories. This study does not claim to be an oral history but draws from oral history.

Phases of Mentoring. Kram (1983) divides mentor relationships into four phases with turning points between each phase: initiation, cultivation, separation, and redefinition. Generally, the initiation phase lasts six to 12 months and cultivation two to five years, with no general timeframe for separation and redefinition (Bullis & Bach, 1989; Kram, 1983).

Plan, Do, Check, Act (PDCA) Cycle. Also known as the Shewhart Cycle, involves the following (Tompkins, 2005):

- *Plan:* develop a quality improvement project
- *Do:* introduce a small-scale change to test the improvement
- *Check:* determine whether the anticipated improvement actually happened and to what extent
- *Act:* introduce broader more permanent changes based on the improvement results

Sensei. Pronounced "sen-say-ee". A mentor from the Japanese Toyota plant. Though sensei is a Japanese word, the term is not specific to Toyota, and a sensei does not have to be Japanese. However, in this study, the word usually refers to a Japanese employee within Toyota mentoring an American Toyota employee.

TMMK. An abbreviation for Toyota Motor Manufacturing Kentucky, which was expanded from the Toyota Georgetown plant.

Assumptions, Limitations, and Delimitations

I assumed that participants answered the questions to the best of their abilities and did not purposefully answer falsely. I believe this is a fair assumption given that the participants were videotaped and audiotaped. I also assume that many of these participants may not have thought about or discussed these items recently and therefore may not recall exact details of each event.

This study's participants are witnesses to a very unique time in history: when a global automaker made a significant footprint in America and the Japanese began significant business ventures within the United States. The primary limitation of the study involves the participants and their memories because these events are so far in the past. Participants may not remember details such as timing, specific individuals, or other exact details of a story with complete accuracy. Thus, limitations will be within specific verbatim details and not necessarily the stories themselves, hence, the context of the stories should be accurate (Yow, 2014).

Concerning delimitations, the research focused on mentor relationships of TMMK because it was the first fully owned American Toyota facility. The leaders within this case study came from outside Toyota (most commonly from other American automotive companies), meaning mentors most likely helped them understand the Toyota way. Due to the nature of executive and mid-level management, the participant pool was small. Additionally, since the events used in this study took place in the 1980s, many of the individuals involved are no longer living or unavailable. Though this study will capture oral histories as a means, the analysis will be only done on mentor relationships.

Summary

This research study used different qualitative techniques to identify characteristics and the overall process of the mentor relationship in the early years of Toyota in Georgetown, Kentucky. This chapter covered the development of the Toyota Production System (TPS) as a unique blend of Japanese Management and lean production. It discussed the history of Toyota's efforts to establish manufacturing facilities in the United States and the often-unsuccessful efforts of many U.S. firms to adapt the lean production portion of TPS. It argued that a major reason for these failures was U.S. firms' lack of attention to the Japanese management side of TPS, especially one of the key mechanisms for implementing and maintaining the system of cooperation and trust characteristic of Japanese worker-management relationships: that of the sensei or mentor. It defined the site and time period of the case researched in this study—the Toyota Motor Manufacturing Kentucky from 1986-1992—as these were the formative years of one of the most notable and successful efforts to integrate TPS into a U.S. facility.

The following chapter will present a more detailed account of the development of the automobile manufacturing industry, organizational theories, the characteristics of the Toyota Production System, the history of Toyota excursions into the U.S. marketplace, and the dissemination of the lean production side of TPS among U.S. firms. This chapter will also provide a more extended discussion of the scholarly literature on mentorship. Chapter 3 will go into much greater detail about the data gathering and data analysis strategies used in this research project, while Chapter 4 will report the key findings of the research and data analysis efforts. Chapter 5 will highlight the major takeaways from the research project, identify fruitful avenues for future research, and present practical applications for firms wanting to implement TPS.

CHAPTER TWO
LITERATURE REVIEW

The purpose of this study is to learn from the developmental interactions between Japanese senseis (mentors) and early American leaders at Toyota Motor Manufacturing Kentucky (TMMK). These Americans had to learn both the Toyota Production System (TPS) and how to lead within the system, which called for a shift in mass production thinking to a type of thinking that meshed with lean production. Specifically, this research aims at learning why and how these early American leaders transitioned from the initiation phase of the mentor relationship to the cultivation phase, which involves active and transformational participation. This research also presents an understanding of the role that mentoring relationships play in broader organizational change toward lean systems.

Historical Context

While this study focuses specifically on the role of mentoring at TMMK, an appreciation of the relevance of mentoring to the success of TMMK requires an understanding of the enormous changes TPS brought to automobile manufacturing in the United States and globally. To provide this necessary context, this section presents brief historical perspectives of automobile manufacturing in the United States and Japan, the entry of Toyota and TPS into U.S. automobile manufacturing, and the diffusion of TPS beyond Toyota.

United States Automobile Industry

The United States has played a central role in the story of the automobile since its invention in the latter half of the 19th century, and the American automobile industry played a major role in the U.S. economy throughout much of the 20th century. This section covers major highlights of the history of the automobile industry in the United States.

From Craft to Mass Production

The automobile was invented and eventually perfected in Europe in the late 1800s, but by the 1920s the American companies of Ford, General Motors, and Chrysler had emerged as the top companies in the world, creating more cars faster with mass production techniques. During World War II these manufacturers funneled resources into wartime production and automobile production ceased. As post-war demand and production grew globally, Japan became a leading auto making country in the 1980s. The shift from craft production to mass production helped automakers increase output and decrease cost, which made automobiles more affordable for the masses. Toyota did not have the capital investment necessary to compete with the likes of Ford, GM, and Chrysler, and therefore was forced to establish its own unique manufacturing processes and eventually become one of the world's top automakers (History Editors,

2018). In the section below, I present an historical overview outlining initial combustion engine vehicle production to present day vehicle production and movements to transition TPS ideas into other sectors such as healthcare.

Early on, cars were primarily made via craft production—individual components of the vehicles were made by hand and assembled. In most cases, the assembly was in a different location than the actual manufacturing of the parts. Over time, manufacturing techniques shifted from craft to modular production of separate chassis and body, to mass production using unibody construction.

Henry Ford founded the Ford Motor Company in 1903 and subsequently invented the mass moving assembly line in 1913. In 1914 Edward Budd and Joe Ledwinka established the process of unibody vehicle construction, which they sold to many automobile makers, replacing the process of assembling the body in many pieces (History Editors, 2018). The shift from craft production to mass production between 1913 and 1914 resulted in a reduction in manufacturing effort of 62% for engines, 75% for magnetos, and 83% for axles. The result was the capacity to create 750 automobiles in the time and effort it previously took to produce 93 (Womack et al., 2007).

The move from craft to mass production meant that output could keep up with growing demand. Between 1908 and 1929 automobile manufacturing companies dropped from 253 to 44, with the majority (80%) of the market controlled by Ford, General Motors, and Chrysler, emerging as the Big 3 in the 1920s. The mass moving assembly line and all-steel unibody construction were two of the greatest improvements to the automobile industry and have come to be known as the *Budd-Ford approach* to automobile manufacturing. This approach essentially led to today's car manufacturing plants, mass production techniques, and finally to the global auto industry (Aoki, 2015).

The Budd-Ford approach led to additional savings through economies of scale. Economy of scale is the relationship between plant size and the lowest possible cost of the product, meaning as the output increases in the factory, typically the cost of the actual product is reduced. Having automation, decreasing downtime through the assembly line, and standardizing to the unibody construction with the assembly line improved economies of scale. Thus, many manufacturers throughout the globe adopted the Budd-Ford approach (Aoki, 2015).

The U.S. Production System

In the United States, price control programs were instituted in the 1940s, 1950s, and 1970s. Oligopolistic pricing occurred in which corporations like General Motors had a target rate of return and utilized *cost-plus pricing*. Cost-plus pricing is essentially adding profit to the cost of goods sold to arrive at a selling price in contrast to allowing the market to drive the selling price. The American automobile industry essentially mass-produced vehicles, keeping the line running regardless of cost, even if this meant reworking defects later. This thinking, coupled with various policy changes, market changes, and other intervening factors, was eventually to lead to a sixty-year sustained loss of market share to foreign countries like Japan (Tansey & Raju, 2017).

Though Henry Ford realized that every time he could

drop prices his cars would be available to more people, that was not necessarily how the industry worked at the time. In spite of the 1933 National Industrial Recovery Act (which was declared unconstitutional in 1935), the reality within the industry manifested itself via the timing of price increases that was coordinated across American firms. This essentially resulted in all cars being priced more or less the same. GM would lead the way, and other manufacturers would change prices accordingly at the time model changes were announced. In the same way, the Big 3, followed by the rest of the U.S. automobile industry, colluded around other policies, including warrantees and financing (Tansey & Raju, 2017).

Additionally, with the security of cost-plus pricing and the big companies having large amounts of cash, the American industry was not really focused on cutting costs the way Toyota and other smaller companies were. This led to the American automobile industry wasting money through wasted time, inferior products, and rework, the cost of which was essentially passed on to the customer due to the nature of cost-plus pricing. If production costs went up, companies could simply raise prices, while selling more cars in a growing market (Tansey & Raju, 2017).

By 1959 the automobile industry had essentially re-organized production systems, and large multi-operation complexes were dismantled and streamlined. Then, smaller homogeneous plants consisted of workers having similar jobs using similar production technologies that fed multiple final assembly plants. An unintentional result of this restructuring of the industry meant that everyone in the plant would share a grievance by one worker—or at least the majority of workers in the plant would have a vested interest in the grievance. This gave unions and union leaders significantly more power to pursue grievances with vigor. Figure 1 shows authorized versus unauthorized strikes in the U.S. auto industry between 1946 and 1979 (Zetka, 1995).

Figure 1

United Auto Workers Strikes 1946–1979

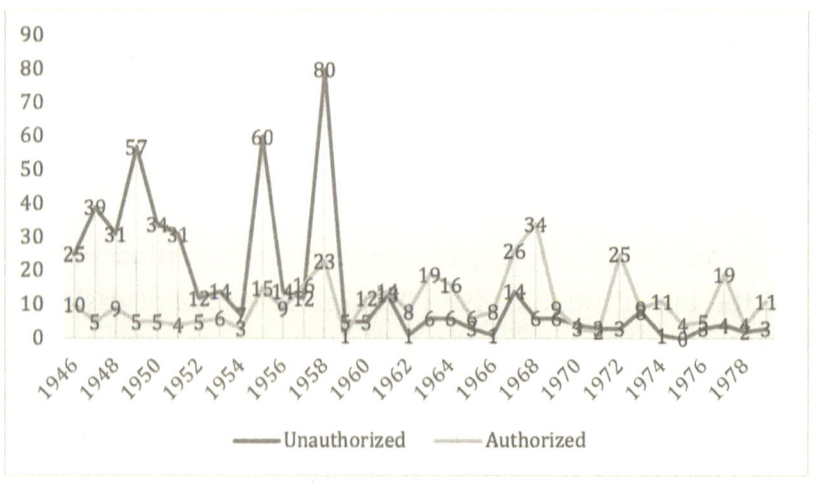

Note. *New York Times* and the *Wall Street Journal* (various years) found in Zetka (1995).

By the 1970s, as energy prices rose, the market demand for small, energy-efficient cars increased and consumers began turning to foreign-made cars because the U.S. was not producing fuel-efficient small cars. The same thinking that drove cost-plus pricing hindered the American auto industry from producing small fuel-efficient cars because smaller cars would cut into profits. This thinking resulted in lost market share to foreign companies as consumers began turning to foreign-made cars because the U.S. was not producing fuel-efficient small cars. Thus, not only did American companies not have fuel-efficient cars but they had also created a production system riddled with waste that could not be passed on to consumers forever.

In 1986, Jim Womack led a research study that resulted in the book *The Machine that Changed the World*, which described lean production versus mass production. While surveying the General Motors plant in Massachusetts, the researchers experienced a classic mass-production environment with all its dysfunctions. Indirect workers—meaning employees who did not work directly on the automobiles—were all over the facility as housekeepers, machine repairers, inventory runners, and other nonvalue added employees. Inventory was piled up between workstations to make up for the uneven distribution of work throughout the line. Some workers were working furiously to catch up, while others were using their waiting time by reading newspapers and taking extra smoke breaks. Additionally, when a part was deemed defective, it was simply tossed into the trash and workers used the next part instead (Womack et al., 2007)

Inventory buffers existed before paint operations and from paint to final assembly. These buffers meant that paint, for example, would always be busy and not slow down the process due to the inefficiencies and uneven distribution of work. The end of the production line mirrored the rest of production: "finished" cars that weren't really finished due to defects needing repair before shipping to the customers (Womack et al., 2007).

The Role of the Automobile in the U.S. Society and Economy

In the 1920s, the American love affair with the automobile gave rise to the petroleum, steel, and other industries, while stimulating outdoor recreation, tourism, and, above all, commuting, which in turn created suburban America. By 1927, Ford's Model T alone had sold 15 million units, making the personal automobile a reality for many (History Editors, 2018). Legislation and research over the next three decades led to the Highway Act of 1956, also known as the Interstate Highway Act. This act authorized the construction of 40,000 miles of national highways over 13 years, with projected costs of over $30 billion. This led to an increase in the trucking industry and accelerated the mass movement of city residents to the suburbs (Riggs, 2015). By 1980, 87.2% of American households owned at least one automobile, and 95% of domestic car sales were for replacement (History Editors, 2018).

The Challenges of the 1970s

By the 1970s, with many more Americans living in the suburbs, highways existing throughout the country and nearly all automobile sales being replacement sales, the resistance of the auto giants to small fuel-efficient cars created the perfect storm for the rise of Japanese auto manufacturing. In October of 1973, the OPEC oil embargo—a ban on the trade of oil to the United States and other countries by the supplier nations Saudi Arabia, Iraq, Iran, and Kuwait—caused gas prices to jump over 40%. This eventually led to a national calling to reduce energy reliance on foreign nations (Riggs, 2015). All these conditions helped give rise to a demand for smaller and more fuel-efficient vehicles. Because of the Big 3's pricing structure and lack of small automobile models, this demand created a vacuum that exporting countries like Japan could fill. Between 1978 and 1984 Detroit alone lost 180,000 manufacturing jobs, and its population declined from 1.8 million in 1950 to 700,000 today (High, 2019).

Toyota Motor Company

The foundation of Toyota dates back to 1918 with an automatic loom for spinning and weaving. Taiichi Ohno, the "father of the Toyota Production System," joined Toyoda Loom Works as an engineering graduate in 1932, and then three years later Kiichiro Toyota founded Toyota Motor Corporation, a spin-off of Toyoda Loom Works. In 1939 Toyota employed about 10,000 people, but after World War II, only about 3,700 got their jobs back because of partially destroyed plants and a lack of raw materials (Cars that made history, 2019). In 1950, Ohno was sent to study American manufacturing methods in U.S. automobile factories, which he hoped to take back to Japan. Because Toyota did not have sufficient capital needed for the economies of scale characteristic of the traditional Ford-Budd approach, Ohno was forced to modify that approach as a way of reducing waste and inventory to increase cash position. Essentially, this is when the Japanese Toyota Production System began (Holweg, 2007).

Taiichi Ohno understood his capital constraints were

significant compared to the likes of Ford and General Motors, so he needed to adapt the concept of mass production. Toyoda and Ohno applied knowledge of the automatic loom, which entailed stopping the line to avoid product waste as the loom machine was down. In other words, instead of keeping the assembly line moving to produce as many units as possible, which was common for the Ford-Budd approach, Toyota stopped the line as defects were identified and built quality into the process.

This way of manufacturing yielded a large variety of cars in small volumes with a common-sense approach of high quality, standardization, and just-in-time inventory management. In other words, Toyota couldn't afford the high inventory levels U.S. auto firms were producing to keep the economies of scale of the high-investment machines. Over the next few decades, Taiichi Ohno refined the small-lot production with economies of scale, evolving Toyota's approach to manufacturing, combined with a Japanese-style approach to management, as defined in Chapter 1 and discussed in more detail later in this chapter, which would eventually influence the American automobile industry under the guise of TPS (Holweg, 2007).

Toyota Production System

The Toyota Production System (TPS) is a manufacturing system that increases productivity and efficiency, eliminating waste. TPS, designed by Toyota's Taiichi Ohno, avoids wastes such as excess inventory, overproduction, motion, transportation, waiting, defects and rework. TPS also integrates just-in-time, Kanban, and production smoothing. Sometimes referred to as Lean, the Toyota Production System was studied prior to but largely made popular in the book *The Machine that Changed the World*.(Toyota Production System, 2013).

In the book, *The Machine that Changed the World*, James Womack, Daniel Jones, and Daniel Roos (2007) describe the Toyota Production System of the 1980s. As part of their research, the authors toured the Takaoka plant in Toyota city, which was built in 1948. Between 1948 and 1980 Toyota was not considered a high-tech facility, although it did have welding and painting robots. However, compared to GM the plant had hardly any nonvalue added employees—housekeepers, troubleshooters, or inventory managers. Essentially, every worker they saw was adding value to the actual automobiles. Space between workstations was minimal, meaning face-to-face communication was easier and stockpiling inventory did not happen (Womack et al., 2007).

Tasks were evenly balanced, resulting in a smooth distribution of work among the workforce. When defects were found they were tagged so that quality control could do a root cause analysis to determine why the defect occurred. Quality control issued new, replacement parts, while GM simply threw the parts away and did no root cause analysis. Similarly, as problems were identified and workers needed assistance, they called for help using an *andon* cord—andon is a Japanese word for light (Womack et al., 2007).

At the end of the line, nearly every car was taken directly to transport for shipping to the customer. This stood in stark contrast to the likes of General Motors, where most cars needed re-working to fix defects. Similarly, there was no buffer before or after the paint booth operation because of the even distribution of work and the predictability of tasks. Most notably, the workforce worked harder, but the sense of purpose and morale was significantly higher than that of the GM workforce. To elaborate, Table 1 shows the differences in assembly time between the GM Framingham plant and the Toyota Takaoka plant (Womack et al., 2007).

Table 1

General Motors Framingham Assembly Plant Versus Toyota Takaoka Assembly Plant, 1986

	GM Framingham	Toyota Takaoka
Gross assembly hours per car	40.7	18.0
Adjusted assembly hours per car	31	16
Assembly defects per 100 cars	130	45
Assembly space per car	8.1	4.8
Average inventories of parts	2 weeks	2 hours

Note. Adapted From Womack, J. P., Jones, D. T., & Roos, D. (2007). *The machine that changed the world.* Simon and Schuster. .

Toyota Manufacturing Comes to the United States

Toyota gained worldwide attention in 1973 when the Arab oil embargo resulted in an oil crisis, which had far-reaching consequences on the global automobile market. This resulted in Japanese and other imports becoming nearly three percent of the American market (Treece, 2013). This was in part due to their higher quality small fuel-efficient vehicles, compared to "hasty, ill-planned and poorly executed attempts" to make small cars by the U.S. auto industry, particularly by Ford and General Motors (Treece, 2013, p. 1).

Figure 2
General Motors and Toyota Learning at and From NUMMI

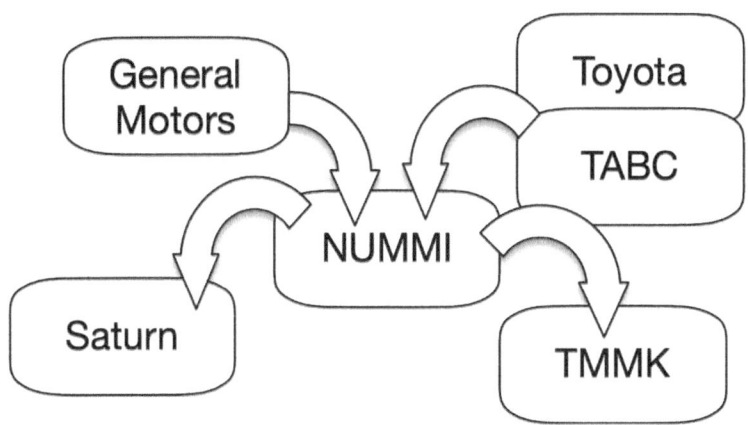

Figure 2 above, though over-simplified, demonstrates that Toyota, via its initial factory in the United States—Toyota Auto Body California (TABC)—partnered with General Motors to form the New United Motor Manufacturing, Inc. (NUMMI). A few short years later, General Motors opened the Saturn Corporation and Toyota began construction of TMMK, both taking advantage of the unique opportunity to learn from each other.

In 1974, after a two-year contract with the previous owners, Toyota purchased operations of what is now Toyota Auto Body California, Inc. (TABC) to produce truck beds (Toyota, 2012). Gary Convis, former executive vice president at Toyota, stated: "TABC laid the foundation for Toyota in the United States. . . . The success of TABC's team members and suppliers certainly paved the way for North American expansion" (Hanson, 2007, p. 1). Using TABC, Toyota and General Motors jointly formed the New United Motor Manufacturing, Inc. (NUMMI) in Freemont, California.

Stemming from TABC, Toyota and General Motors next formed a joint venture called NUMMI in 1983, which was located in the recently closed General Motors plant in Freemont, California. The plant employed mostly GM people, and thus, to a great extent, started with the traditional GM culture. The main goals of the venture for Toyota were a rapid entry to the U.S. market and an opportunity to learn how to work with an American workforce (Inkpen, 2005). For General Motors, the goals were to learn TPS first-hand and produce a small car (Wilms, 1996). General Motors also wanted its managers to personally witness how the Japanese operated in terms of teamwork, high quality, and low-cost (Sherman, 1994). Within one year, the NUMMI plant went from an old "bad" culture producing the worst quality products within GM to the best quality producer in the company, with a notably good culture of mutual trust and respect (Shook, 2010).

Toyota was responsible for design, operations, and production and thus it managed NUMMI, taking full responsibility for mentoring the American workforce of 2,500 employees (Wilms, 1996). The joint venture became a great opportunity for General Motors to learn from Toyota and take relevant aspects of TPS and Japanese manufacturing and management back to General Motors. Unfortunately, this proved easier said than done. GM managers, who were expected to eventually mentor TPS-like systems, were assigned to NUMMI and simply told to learn as much as possible in as short a time as possible. Though they tried, many on their return to GM came to realize that even if they understood the tools, they did not know how to integrate them into an existing organizational culture (Inkpen, 2005). Nonetheless, this collaboration produced one of GM's best attempts at competing with the Japanese, its Saturn facility at Spring Hill, Tennessee.

With Saturn, GM embarked on the largest one-time investment in the history of the United States automobile industry: a $5 billion initiative to compete with Japanese and other automobile imports, which created 6,000 jobs directly, plus an estimated 15,000 more indirectly (Sherman, 1994). General Motors then attempted to spread aspects of the Toyota Production System from what it had learned at NUMMI throughout Spring Hill. Facing shrinking profits and market share, General Motors needed to reestablish both its power and influence within the automotive market. By April 1992, GM's new subsidiary, Saturn, had been awarded the highest rating for mechanical reliability by *Consumer Reports*, and J.D. Powers ranked Saturn third in customer satisfaction behind only luxury brands Lexus and Infiniti. Saturn stood apart from both General Motors and the rest of the American automobile industry as it focused on integrated business systems and an enlightened workforce (Sherman, 1994). To operationalize Saturn's philosophy, it had compensation packages for Saturn's employees that included lifetime employment and production-based bonuses (Sherman, 1994).

At Saturn's peak, it emulated Toyota—paralleling the NUMMI plant. This put General Motors in a position to compete with the Japanese directly from both a product and an organizational culture standpoint. Eventually, though, Saturn ended up closing its doors and becoming just another GM plant. The Saturn brand and management style ceased to exist due to problems with quality, profitability, management systems, reduction of bonuses, and a lack of clear roles and responsibilities, coupled with General Motors specific issues including culture, leadership, and labor-management relations (Aaker, 1994; Sherman, 1994). These problems might have been avoided with a more long-term approach that used experienced mentors at the executive leadership levels of General Motors similar to the approach Toyota took to leadership at Georgetown.

After Toyota achieved its objective of learning how to work with an American workforce at NUMMI, its next venture was its first fully owned and operated plant that would build a car in the United States located in Georgetown, Kentucky. Toyota leaders from Japan were worried, as were American dealers, that an American workforce might not be able to produce the same quality vehicles that were currently coming from Japan (Chappell, 2007). Toyota moved forward, however, after its initial experience at NUMMI. In 1985, Toyota announced Toyota Georgetown, Kentucky, as its first fully owned and operated facility in America. Ground was broken in 1986, the power train plant was announced in 1987, and the first car at the location was produced in 1988 (Company History, n.d.).

At Georgetown, later named Toyota Motor Manufacturing Kentucky (TMMK), "developing human infrastructure was TMC's [Toyota Motor Company's] foremost priority," as evidenced by several factors (Mishina & Takeda, 1995, p. 3). First, Toyota's construction started the same year it began hiring, which allowed Toyota just as much time to develop "people infrastructure" as to develop "operational infrastructure" (Mishina & Takeda, 1995, p. 3). Second, the production line for the Camry—which was already being mass-produced in Japan—was replicated in Georgetown. This decision gave everyone more time and energy to focus on developing people rather than creating a completely new production line. Third, Toyota purposefully used a slow ramp-up schedule, which allowed time for employees to gradually learn and become successful, as opposed to starting the production line at full capacity right away. As the Japanese were learning the American workforce and market—both at Honda and Toyota—American companies like Ford and General Motors were trying to compete against the Japanese quality and small cars. It was becoming evident that the Toyota Production System produced superior results (Mishina & Takeda, 1995).

The initial construction of Toyota at Georgetown was controversial in the community, drawing over 800 residents to the Georgetown city council meeting to approve the initial plans for Toyota (Chappell, 2007). Three years later, when Toyota went to the same city council to obtain approval for expansion, virtually no one came to the meeting, signaling no controversy and that Toyota had achieved community approval (Chappell, 2007). Decades later, TMMK grew to be the largest vehicle manufacturing facility for Toyota in the world. This stands in stark contrast to the NUMMI and Saturn plants, which both eventually closed. Additionally, in 2017, Toyota invested $1.3 billion to upgrade the assembly plant in Kentucky, solidifying its commitment to production within the United States (Vlasic, 2017). In 2007, Gary Convis, the first American president at TMMK, stated: "We began to understand after a number of years that we had benefited from some inspired leadership in those early years [at TMMK]. It makes you realize how important this all was to Toyota" (Chappell, 2007, p. 102). From the start of TMMK, TPS continued to diffuse throughout North America, as new suppliers worked closely with Toyota.

The Diffusion of TPS in the United States

As Figure 3 demonstrates, the general spread of the Toyota Production System moved from Toyota in Japan to Toyota's joint venture with General Motors via Toyota Auto Body California to Toyota's first plant in Kentucky, TMMK. The diffusion of TPS generally occurred from Toyota to General Motors, then to Toyota's suppliers, then to other manufacturing operations and, eventually, to the healthcare sector facilitated by academic research and professional consultants.

As Figure 3 depicts, due to the emphasis eluded to in the historical accounts, the focus of this research rests with the mentor relationships, which were paramount during the initial years of TMMK between the Japanese and early American leaders. Toyota in Japan started TABC in the United States, which expanded into the joint venture at NUMMI. NUMMI then influenced the rest of General Motors while helping Toyota expand further into the United States via what eventually became TMMK. TMMK influenced Toyota's suppliers to improve the Toyota supply chain. Many other manufacturers interested in the Toyota Production System began to learn from Toyota's suppliers (as well as from Toyota and General Motors). This section describes the diffusion of TPS through suppliers, academia, consultants, and healthcare.

Figure 3
Transferring Knowledge of TPS From Japanese Sensei to Early U.S. Leaders at TMMK

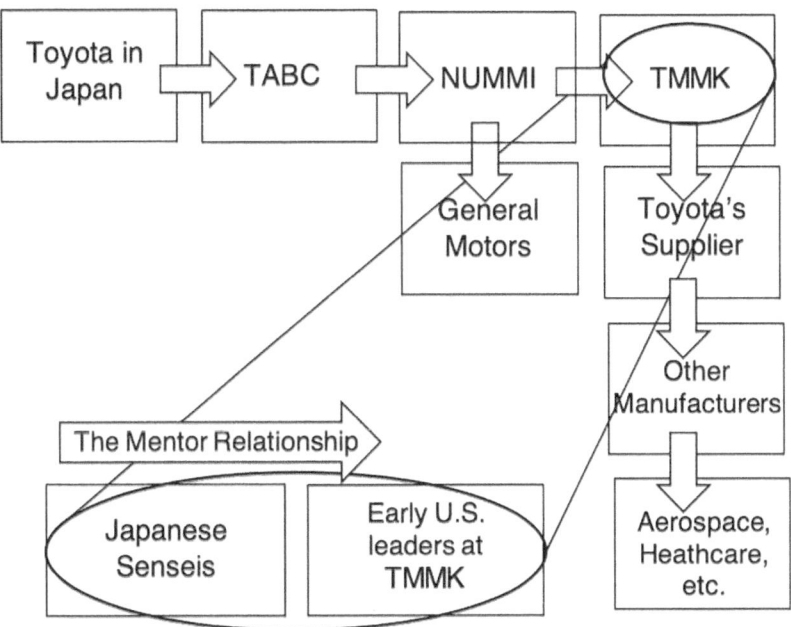

Toyota Supplier Support Center

Early on at TMMK, Toyota understood the need to develop suppliers and create a knowledge-sharing network. The Toyota Supplier Support Center (TSSC) was established in 1992 to provide TPS training to its supplier base. The operation of TSSC was based on Toyota's internal Operations Management Consulting Division (OMCD) in Japan. OMCD had been created to allow Toyota's employees to solve complex problems through teaching, training, and coaching, as they were tasked with facilitating, leading, and training on improvement efforts (Spear & Bowen, 1999). At OMCD, a group of highly skilled Toyota consultants assisted with solving operational problems that impacted both Toyota internally and its suppliers (Dyer & Nobeoka, 2000). The improvement activities, also called *kaizen* events by OMCD and later TSSC, were characterized by the following (Kato & Smalley, 2010):

- Establishing a topic, theme, or general subject matter for improvement
- Implementing improvement activities
- Adapting as needed and repeating implementation until the targeted operational and business results were achieved
- Presenting a summary of results
- Conducting a final evaluation of comments by Toyota's OMCD department

Complex problems were solved via kaizen events, the Japanese word for "continuous improvement," led by the internal Toyota consultants and leaders from TSSC/OMCD. Toyota did not ask suppliers to adopt TPS completely but only those aspects of the process that directly affected Toyota. The reason for this was described by one of the first general managers of TSSC, Hajime Ohba, who recognized the discrepancy between traditional North American organizations and Toyota: "It takes a very long time and tremendous commitment to implement the Toyota Production System. In many cases, it takes a total cultural and organizational change. Many U.S. firms have management systems that contradict where you need to go" (Dyer & Nobeoka, 2000, p. 354). Toyota did not—and still does not—target entire organizational systems when working with suppliers; rather, it targets those processes that directly impact the company.

Even though Toyota never demanded it, leaders within supply organizations learned the kaizen methodology for solving problems and began to apply it to solve their own internal issues. Unfortunately, a kaizen event is only one part of TPS. Since many of the suppliers did not understand the totality of TPS, they set out on a journey to become lean, attempting to simply copy Toyota kaizen events while neglecting other important aspects of TPS, including the mentor relationship.

Academia Promotes Kaizen

The business and academic worlds began to take note of the Toyota Production System in 1965 when the concepts of Kanban, an element of just-in-time inventory, were introduced to Toyota's suppliers (Holweg, 2007). Then in 1988, John F. Krafcik published "Triumph of the Lean Production System" in MIT's *Sloan Management Review*, which carried significant clout throughout the automobile industry. In many ways, it marked the beginning of what has become known as the lean movement in the United States, which was studied extensively by the academic world. Krafcik's argues that it is not a vehicle's country of origin that determines its quality-to-cost ratio—a common myth at that time—but whether or not lean production philosophies are in place to enable manufacturers to produce high-quality, low-cost models (Krafcik, 1988).

Krafcik's article was shortly followed by *The Machine That Changed the World* (Womack et al., 2007), the result of an extensive MIT study that compared and contrasted the thinking, philosophies, and management behind mass production and lean production. This thorough, five-year, $5 million, 14-country study promoted and popularized the Toyota Production System. This research and book correctly predicted the triumph of lean philosophies and production over conventional mass production and the application of lean into a variety of industries outside the automobile industry, including healthcare. After its publication and the successes of lean manufacturing, improvement professionals became almost obsessed with Toyota, trying to understand how to transform their companies into lean organizations.

Professionalization: Experts and Consultants

The use of Toyota-style tools and kaizen-event-based approaches led to many organizations attempting to emulate Toyota, which in turn has led to an abundance of successful professionals who have learned, refined, and elaborated on the kaizen event-based pathways to becoming lean. Professionalization includes "the resting of formal education and of legitimation in a cognitive base produced by university specialists; and the growth and elaboration of professional networks that span organizations and across which new models diffuse rapidly" (DiMaggio & Powell, 1983, p. 152). Professionalization of tools—kanban, andon, standardized work, workplace organization, and so forth—surrounded the kaizen event that was being rapidly diffused throughout North America, but many of these adaptations neglected the management systems and cultural changes required for the success of these tools (Dyer & Nobeoka, 2000; Kaplan et al., 2014).

The professionals performing project facilitation and leadership development—like OMCD within its own organization or within a lean organization—comprised the vast majority of lean practitioners and professionals in the early years of lean diffusion and still do today in most, if not all, industries. Senior leaders within aspiring lean organizations look to these professionals, including both internal employees and external consultants, to initiate lean transformation. As Liker and Convis (2011) explain,

> Traditionally, the role of a lean consultant is to run a project and deliver an action plan. . . . They claim to have expertise in lean methods and guarantee that they can eliminate waste. . . . Kaizen blitzes (another term for kaizen events) and acting fast for results is the antithesis of good lean practice, which is based on finding the root causes and the best solutions and sharing lessons for continuous improvement. (pp. 250-251)

Yet due to the professionalization of an event-based and/or tools-based approach to lean, both manufacturing and healthcare generally started with kaizen events to focus on eliminating waste and reducing cost.

Healthcare

After the widespread diffusion of lean into primarily the manufacturing sector using the professionalized, event-based, tools-based approach, early adopters of lean in healthcare looked to manufacturing for solutions to organizational and process problems. *Going Lean in Healthcare* (Institute for Healthcare Improvement, 2005), an initial publication of the institute about lean healthcare transformation, cites the results of 175 Rapid Process Improvement Workshops, a seven-week cycle including an initial one-week kaizen event, which showed positive changes in inventory, productivity, floor space utilization, lead time, and set up time (Institute for Healthcare Improvement, 2005, p. 4). Each cycle includes lean training, understanding the current state, defining a future state (based on the ideal), implementing the steps to get to the future state, testing and standardizing the new process, and reporting the results (Toussaint & Gerard, 2010). This is essentially the OMCD/TSSC approach to lean as focused on process changes, but it ignores cultural and management system changes.

Though an event-based approach to lean transformation has resulted in improvements—many of which have been widely documented, shared, and expanded upon—simply reengineering processes has resulted in many failures that have gone undocumented and unpublished. Many lean organizations learned from individuals who had mastered kaizen events, but these individuals were not necessarily leaders who had mastered organizational transformation. Very few people have experience with high levels of Toyota leadership compared to the number who have experienced kaizen events. Understanding how adaptations of the Toyota Production System have spread over the last 25 to 30 years casts light on why so many organizations have not been successful at transformation. As mentioned earlier, not only is restructuring work necessary but also creating a culture of mutual trust and respect between employees, management, and the community is key. In other words, "transformation requires using lean as part of a comprehensive management system in concert with institutional culture change and new leadership approaches to all aspects of healthcare delivery" (Kaplan et al., 2014, p. 927).

Organizational Theory and Change

Organizational theories, including Scientific and Quality Management, influenced business leaders in Japan, including those at Toyota. Taylorism or Scientific Management became popular around 1910 as Taylor recognized that industrialization meant more complex organizations and the need to remove some complexity through standardization. About a decade later, Quality Management Theory built upon Taylorism and Statistical Process Control leading to the Total Quality Management movement of the 1960s and 70s in Japan and later in the 1980s in the United States (Tompkins, 2005).

By the time Toyota Georgetown came into existence, Toyota's Japanese leaders realized that Georgetown demanded a unique combination of Western management and the Toyota Production System (Ouchi, 1981; Sullivan, 1983). The Toyota Production System in Georgetown, Kentucky, became a blend of Japanese management, U.S. management, mass production, and Toyota-specific manufacturing systems. Before beginning Georgetown, Toyota had the opportunity to plan how the unique blend of manufacturing techniques and Japanese management could be instilled into the American workforce. Toyota's approach also seemed to uniquely blend Taylor's scientific management and Deming/Juran's total quality management. Additionally, since 1974 the Japanese had already experienced western management and the

American workforce at Toyota's acquired auto-body plant in California and, nine years later, through a joint venture with General Motors, also in California.

Scientific Management

Frederick W. Taylor (1856-1915) is the father of Scientific Management or the theory of organizational effectiveness, which essentially states that to increase output organizations should systemize work processes. This systemization is done by "dividing work into narrowly defined tasks, determining the 'one best way' to perform each task, train workers in the 'one best way,' measure their performance, and offering economic incentives for surpassing daily production quotas" (Tompkins, 2005, p. 67).

Taylor recognized that industrialization meant increasing the size and complexity of organizations, which had its own set of problems to solve. Taylor concluded that the structure and practice of management must change to meet the new demands of industrialization. At this time, workers generally took direction from a decentralized management with essentially no middle management responsible for planning, measuring, or cost accounting. As a result of not having divided work with standard instructions and performance targets, upper management could not plan productivity, incentives, and discipline based on realistic productivity and performance standards. This current state of industry led Taylor to conceptualize what has become known as Scientific Management (Tompkins, 2005).

Taylor, troubled by poverty and other social issues, recognized that both owners and workers could work together to increase output and wealth for all, which would translate into more money for owners, higher wages for workers, and lower prices for customers. With everyone focused on one best way, organizations could improve socioeconomic conditions by eliminating waste and increasing profits.

Taylorism became widely known in 1910-1911 when the Eastern Railroad Company needed to increase its rates to remain profitable, which ended up before the Interstate Commerce Commission as the Eastern Rate Case in 1910. Using scientific management, the commission determined that the railroad could eliminate waste to find the needed savings, which eliminated the need to increase rates. Thus, the elimination of waste via scientific management was demonstrated to potentially save the railroad a million dollars a day, which made Taylor and scientific management a household name (Tompkins, 2005).

The purpose of scientific management was to increase productivity by determining a fair day's work and aligning tasks and incentives with that fair day's work instead of guessing what productivity should be. Scientific management included all aspects of production and was implemented in a prescriptive way, usually over three years, and included the following (Tompkins, 2005):

1. The 3 Rights: Right place, right time, for the right tools and materials
2. Task setting: Written instructions for each task for workers
3. Time study: Determining and specifying the exact time for each task or work element
4. Incentives: Providing economic incentives to

complete tasks in the determined time

Toyota is known to teach its employees how to see and similarly eliminate waste, and this mindset has become a given of the Toyota Production System. Unfortunately, though, in the late 1940s, academia began to demean Taylor and discredit his contribution to organizational theory and his impact on improving organizations, largely because of his opposition to unions, obsession with control, and limited understanding of psychology. Additionally, scientific management in general seemed to dehumanize workers by focusing on the simplification and standardization of work tasks. Even though Taylor clearly understood and had a sincere concern for the wellbeing and treatment of workers, as demonstrated by his writings and his biography, the human side of production seemed to be lacking in scientific management (Tompkins, 2005).

Quality Management Theory

Quality Management Theory built upon scientific management and began in the 1920s with Walter Shewhart's concept of Statistical Process Control (SPC), eventually evolving into the theory of quality management in the 1950s. Quality Management or Total Quality Management contributed significantly to the success of Japanese firms like Toyota in the 1960s and 1970s, eventually being widely recognized in the 1980s by Americans. Statistical process control, as opposed to quality control by inspection, involves collecting data on variations in quality to eliminate the causes of variation at different steps in the production process. Since statistical process control relies on preventing quality errors, as opposed to inspection and correction, it is more logical and cost-effective. Additionally, process quality control means less inventory and improved cash flow (Tompkins, 2005).

Between the 1920s and the 1980s and the start of Toyota Georgetown, SPC evolved from a process technique to an overall management philosophy known as Total Quality Control or Total Quality Management. In the 1950s, at General Electric, Armand Feigenbaum emphasized four sets of activities for total quality control and the utilization of statistical process control as a management function (Tompkins, 2005):

1. Planning of controls for new/modified products before production starts
2. Controlling incoming/purchased materials
3. Product control within machines and processes
4. Conducting analyses of process problems

But even though statistical process control saved millions of dollars from reduced inspection and rework during the Second World War in the United States, postwar American industry, by and large, did not adopt SPC and reverted to quality control via inspection and rework. Deming, an Iowa native, Ph.D., and engineer learned statistical process control from Shewhart and began giving courses on statistical process control for engineers, inspectors, and others during wartime production. After the war, with a dwindling American audience, Deming's teachings rooted in Shewhart, piqued the interest of audiences in Japan (Tompkins, 2005).

In Japan, Deming reinforced Schewhart's teachings

of Plan-Do-Check-Act cycle used to implement continuous improvement to immediate work processes. The PDCA Cycle, also known as the Shewhart Cycle, involves the following:

- Plan: develop a quality improvement project
- Do: introduce a small-scale change to test the improvement
- Check: determine whether the anticipated improvement actually happened and to what extent
- Act: introduce broader more permanent changes based on the improvement results

Essentially, Deming and Joseph Juran, an American quality control expert, introduced Japanese executives to aspects of total quality control. It was not until Deming appeared in an American documentary in 1980 did American manufacturing give serious thought to what was now being labeled as Total Quality Management, which primarily emerged from ideas of espoused by Juran and Japanese manufacturers' responses to Deming's more limited statistical methods (Tsutsui, 1996). Often over credited with the quality movement after his television appearance, ideas demonstrating a philosophy reaching beyond statistical process control were frequently attributed to Deming in addition to the following philosophical points (Tsutsui, 1996 and Tompkins, 2005, p. 341):

1. Create consistency of purpose for improvement of product and service
2. Adopt the new philosophy
3. Cease dependence on mass inspection

4. End the practice of awarding business on price tag alone
5. Improve constantly and forever the system of production and service
6. Institute training
7. Institute leadership
8. Drive out fear
9. Break down barriers between staff areas
10. Eliminate slogans, exhortations, and targets for the workforce
11. Eliminate numerical quotas for the workforce and numerical goals for people in management
12. Remove barriers to pride of workmanship
13. Institute vigorous program of education and self-improvement
14. Take action to accomplish the transformation.
15. Building upon Deming, Juran's structural approach to quality management included quality planning (developing what the customer actually wants), quality control (evaluating quality performance against expectations), and quality improvement (bringing quality performance to unprecedented levels via continuous improvement).

Total Quality Management became something of a fad in American companies in the 1980s and 1990s, leading to scholars and practitioners alike generally falling into two schools of thought. The first was that TQM was essentially scientific management plus some humanistic aspects that Taylor was initially missing. The second school of thought was that TQM was a positive contribution to organizations and integrates seemingly more positive aspects of Taylor's scientific management, human resource theory, systems theory, and strategic planning theory as described below (Tompkins, p. 346):

1. Human resource theory: Concepts of trust, involvement, and personal development
2. Systems theory: Management is responsible for managing the organization in a fully integrated manner
3. Strategic planning theory: Visionary leadership and the importance of keeping everyone focused on mission, purpose, and vision

Tompkins further states, "Human resources theory assumes that workers are reservoirs of untapped resources, that they have the capacity to be self-directing and self-controlling, and that organizational success depends on how fully their abilities are developed and utilized" (Tompkins, p. 296). Leaders within organizations can tap into the resources of human capital. However, at Toyota Georgetown in the 1980s, Toyota not only had to develop the workforce, but they had to develop American leaders to develop the workforce at the same time, all within a lean production system with Americans only familiar with mass production. Understanding Toyota's approach to developing leaders to develop others may be essential to understanding the mentor relationships between senseis and the newly hired Americans that were established during the early days at Georgetown.

Leadership in Organizations

Leadership is to accomplish some change in the world that responds to human wants— i.e., the pursuit of happiness (Burns, 2004). To define a leader, the dimensions of leadership must be identified and must exist for the person to be considered a leader (Bowers & Seashore, 1966):

- When two are more people are together in a group
- The (presumed) leader must have behavior which moves the group toward a shared goal
- That behavior must be directed toward another person in the group

The definition of leadership, however, has evolved over the years (Northouse, 2012):

- 1900-1929: emphasis on control, centralization of power, and domination
- 1930s: The emergence of influence over domination
- 1940s: An individual with certain personality traits influencing a group of people
- 1950s: The emergence of theories resulting in what leaders do in groups, how leaders behave, and how leaders influence group effectiveness
- 1960s: Scholarly agreement that leadership is a behavior that influences a group toward shared goals
- 1970s: Leadership as a reciprocal process between leaders and followers
- 1980s: The emergence of themes including do as

the leader wishes; influence; traits; and transformational leadership
- 1990s to the present: the agreement that leadership is an extremely complex concept and the definition will continue to be in flux

As leadership was being studied and defined, leadership practices were also evolving within Japanese businesses, including Toyota, based on the Japanese culture. Japanese businesses, and thus leadership practices, were influenced by Japanese management. With firms in Japan having paternalistic relationships, cooperation, and trust, these cultural norms would presumably impact leadership characteristics at Toyota (Bright, 2005; Ouchi, 1981).

Leadership at Toyota

With Toyota's unique blend of management and production techniques, coupled with the need to hire an American workforce, developing leaders to adapt and implement the Toyota Way was extremely important to the long-term success of Toyota. Katz (1955) argued that organizations should develop leaders by developing skills and creating learning by doing. These skills include technical, human, and conceptual skills, which vary based on the level of leadership and administrative responsibility within the organization.

At lower organizational levels, like frontline team members who may be working on the factory floor, technical skills are of the utmost importance. As leadership progresses from frontline team leadership to higher, more senior levels of leadership, both technical and human skills become more important. Frontline supervisors can help solve operational problems based on technical knowledge, whereas administrative leaders may need less technical knowledge and more human interaction skills to facilitate the improvement and stability needed for organizational success (Katz, 1955). Human interaction skills are important at all levels of the workforce, but technical skills seem less important as leaders are promoted, according to Katz.

Though technical knowledge is important for administrative leaders, Katz tends to downplay it due to the higher importance of both human and conceptual skills at that level (Katz, 1955). Administrative traits needed for higher-level leaders include planning, organization, delegation, follow-up, and overall coordination, among many others (Bowers & Seashore, 1966). Technical skills can be taught, as described in scientific management theory, but farther removed from the frontline the higher the need is for conceptual and human knowledge skills for effective leaders (Katz, 1955). Additionally, "organizations must balance the tendency toward stability... with the need for change" (Mumford et al., 2000, p. 13). Therefore, leaders must learn how to balance scientific management with quality improvement techniques, which involve both technical and human skills. In the case of Toyota Georgetown, Japanese leaders not only had to balance scientific management with quality improvement, but they also had to teach the new American leaders how to do both through mentoring relationships.

The Toyota Production System is characterized on the human relations side by highly productive industrial workgroups, which embed the influence of Japanese management (Aoki, 2015). A study by England (1983) shows that Japanese compared to American workers trust management, help each other more, value working more, and place their company in more of a central role in their lives. The norm for Japanese workers was "high-levels of work effort and commitment; organizational involvement; and cooperation, acceptance, and trust in management policies and practices" (Ouchi, 1981, p. 134).

According to William Ouchi, the author of the highly influential book, *Theory Z: How American Business Can Meet the Japanese Challenge* (1981), Japanese cultural imperatives are different than those of Americans. These imperatives include influence incentives, cooperation, and trust. Thus, the ability to create an industrial workgroup is much easier in Japan than it is in the United States. Industrial workgroups or clans are unifying within the workplace, but are planned within the corporation and functions to regulate employee behavior and social relations (Sullivan, 1983). In American companies, managerial decisions create corporate philosophy, which can potentially create an industrial workgroup. Ouchi theorized that industrial workgroups would increase worker productivity. To summarize our understanding of Japanese management, Takezawa and Whitehill (1981) note the following:

> Japanese improvements during the 1960-76 period seem best accountable, then, as a result of the continuous deliberate efforts by all parties in the total socioeconomic process, particularly in the area of industrial relations. Japanese management, unions, government, workers, and citizens apparently have come to share broader mutual goals, for the attain-

ment of which the parties are prepared to work better together in a spirit of cooperation. (p. 197)

Mentoring: A Developmental Interaction

One of the many problems that organizations face when adapting TPS is executive resistance and misunderstanding of lean management and leadership in a lean environment (Emiliani, 2018; Sherman, 1994). Since other potential problems—such as resource constraints and cultural issues—can be strongly influenced by leadership, understanding how to overcome executive resistance and misunderstanding of TPS is an important aspect of this research. Toyota may have faced a similar problem when it hired leaders from other automotive companies during the initial years at TMMK. Understanding how Toyota deployed senseis to overcome this problem may provide insight into better executive-level coaching and mentoring program design. Toyota's approach at Georgetown included experienced Toyota leaders developing American leaders. During the ramp-up stage U.S. managers employed by Toyota "could witness actions in the context around them, appreciate unexpectedly positive results, and have their coaches make sense of what lay behind these results" (Mishina & Takeda, 1995, p. 3). Thus, an understanding of the sensei-protégé relationship within the context of the TMMK changing culture, management systems, and leadership styles becomes especially important.

The first research question is to identify characteristics of the developmental relationship between early leaders at

TMMK and their Japanese counterparts. In order to research this question, exploring the different types of developmental relationships and the respective characteristics is necessary. Thus, this section explores different types of developmental relationships including coaching, apprenticeship, action learning, and tutoring. Based on the description of mentoring and Toyota's early senseis discussed in the literature, the relationships at TMMK seem to be mentoring relationships. Though we cannot say this with certainty, deeply understanding the different types and characteristics of mentor relationships is essential in understanding the relationships at Toyota and answering the first research question.

The second research question is stated in a way that characterizes the sensei-protégé relationships as mentoring relationships. Kram (1983) identifies the phases of a mentor relationship as initiation, cultivation, separation, and redefinition. This research question specifically aims to identify common actions senseis took to advance mentoring relationships from the initiation phase to the cultivation phase of the relationship. Therefore, understanding the phases of mentoring may provide insight into how the Japanese senseis were able to have an impact on the Americans at Toyota and will be discussed in the later part of this section. Finally, understanding mentorships within the Japanese culture and its organizational benefits in any culture will provide insight into how and why Toyota may have adapted Japanese mentoring to meet the needs of the American workforce. The following section will broadly cover developmental interactions and provide deeper focus on mentoring, as portrayed in Figure 4.

Figure 4

Types of Developmental Interactions

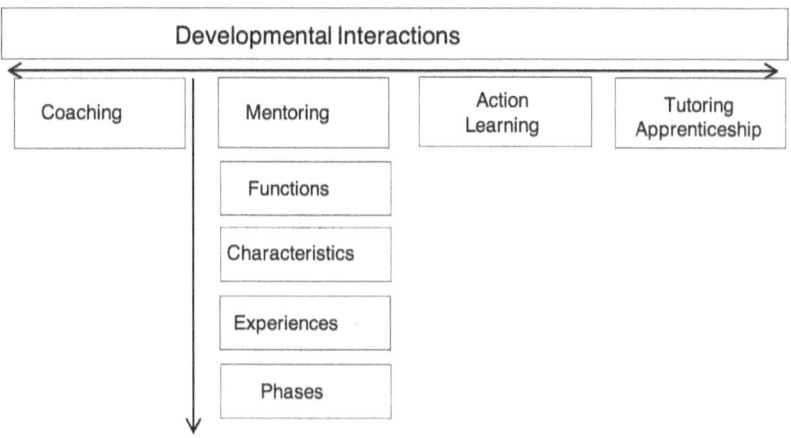

Note. Adapted from *Coghlan & Brydon-Miller, 2014; D'Abate et al., 2003; Riggs, 2015.*

Types of Developmental Interactions

Development of individuals as current or eventual members of the workforce occurs in many different forms depending on the relationship and the objective of the relationship. These relationships can have interactions classified as coaching, mentoring, apprenticeship, action learning, and tutoring, and are known as developmental interactions (D'Abate et al., 2003). Coaching is generally at the executive level with peer-to-peer interactions focused on action. Mentoring, discussed at length in the following section, can be formal or informal, generally matching a more experienced with a less experienced individual. Action learning can occur within both mentoring and coaching relationships focused on solving real problems and taking action. Apprenticeships and tutoring are generally career focused and based on observation. Table 2 shows and defines the categories of developmental interactions as discussed in D'Abate et al. in further detail (Coghlan & Brydon-Miller, 2014; D'Abate et al., 2003; Riggs, 2015).

Table 2

Categories of Developmental Interactions

Category	Definition
Coaching	This interaction is generally associated with the executive level. It often involves a peer-to-peer relationship and is action-oriented.
Mentoring	This relationship may either be formal and structured (generally facilitated by HR) or informal and unstructured. It routinely occurs between a more experienced or senior individual (i.e., the mentor) and a less experienced or less senior individual (i.e., the mentee).
Action Learning	This interaction primarily focuses on real problems, followed by taking action, and then reflection on what has been learned by the results (i.e., an after-action review). It may occur within both coaching and mentoring relationships.
Apprenticeship & Tutoring	This relationship may be either formal or informal and it is generally career-focused. It frequently relies on observation and direct experience.

Note. Adapted from D'Abate, C., Eddy, E., & Tannenbaum, S. (2003). What's in a name? A literature-based approach to understanding mentoring, coaching, and other constructs that describe developmental interactions. *Human Resource Development Review*, 2(4), 360–384. doi.org10.1177/1534484303255033; Dioso-Henson, L. (2012). The effect of reciprocal peer tutoring and non-reciprocal peer tutoring on the performance of students in college Physics. *Research in Education*, 87(1), 34–49. doi.org/10.7227/RIE.87.1.3; and Wendrich, W. (Ed.). (2016). *Archaeology and apprenticeship: Body knowledge, identity, and communities of practice*. University of Arizona Press.

Mentoring

From the review of the literature, it is presumed that

sensei-protégé relationships are most closely aligned with mentor relationships; however, mentoring at Toyota may have included aspects of action learning and coaching. Some have even combined action learning and mentoring into a concept of action mentoring. Therefore, comparing action learning, coaching, and mentoring will help characterize the relationships at Toyota.

"Mentor" is the name given to the coach, counselor, and advisor of Telemachus in Homer's *Odyssey* and the name has evolved into a term that means "a wise and trusted teacher" (Finley et al., 2007; Klauss, 1981; Marrelli, 2004). The role of a mentor often includes that of a father figure and protector in a relationship of mutual trust and affection (Klauss, 1981). The scholarly literature consistently describes mentor as a more experienced individual helping a less experienced one by providing support, acting as a role model, and aiding in skill development (D'Abate, 2010). Similarly, "mentorship," from a business or professional perspective, is defined as a relationship in which one individual assists another professionally with the intent of improving and optimizing work performance (Srivastava & Jomon, 2013).

Like mentor, sensei (pronounced sen-say-ee) is a Japanese word that means "honorable and respected teacher or elder," although its literal meaning is "firstborn." In some Japanese organizations like Toyota, employees are matched with a sensei that is responsible for transferring knowledge, a characteristic of a developmental interaction (Mihut, 2014). It seems that sensei-protégé relationships are closely aligned with mentoring relationships. This section helps identify different types of mentor relationships to further characterize Toyota's sensei-protégé relationships.

If the results suggest that the sensei-protégé relationship is indeed a mentor relationship, understanding the different types of mentor relationships will help further describe the sensei-protégé relationships at Toyota.

Mentoring and Coaching

Coaching and mentoring have many similarities. Coaching, like mentoring, optimizes a junior's knowledge of an organization or profession (Kram, 1983). Typically, both the mentor and the coach suggest strategies to help the protégé achieve aspirations or goals (Kram, 1983). Arguably, coaching may be one aspect or characteristic of mentoring (Kram, 1983; Rosser, 2005). In spite of similarities, however, the two are best understood as different developmental interactions. D'Abate et al. (2003) suggest that coaching focuses on a specific objective or technique, provides feedback, and generally teaches in a short-term setting within the realm of an employee relationship. A mentor tends to work in a long-term setting and focuses on reflexive learning, which is a process of reflectively analyzing and learning from one's experience (D'Abate et al., 2003; Jenkins, 2013). Therefore, a mentor may provide coaching from time to time, but a coach is not necessarily a mentor.

Action Learning and Mentoring

Action learning is common in professional management, education, organizational change, problem solving, and performance improvement. It can take place in teams or individuals, but always involves engaging in learning by doing and doing by learning—the fundamental assumption is that "learning requires action and action requires learning" (Action Learning, para. 3). One key premise is that individuals must change themselves if they expect to change others or an organization. Frequently, action learning requires some form of mentoring or coaching, which between individuals may be characterized by cycles of action and reflection facilitated by the coach or mentor (Coghlan & Brydon-Miller, 2014).

Traditional Mentoring

Traditional mentoring includes both career and psychosocial mentoring, both of which are used in the workplace. Understanding traditional mentoring in more detail, with its specific functions, will help identify in what aspects the sensei-protégé relationship may include or exclude aspects of traditional mentoring. Functions include sponsorship, exposure/visibility, challenging assignments, protecting, role modeling, acceptance/confirmation, counseling, friendship, and coaching. A mentor, from a career standpoint, may prepare the protégé to become a manager, nominate them for desirable projects, recommend for promotions, meet new colleagues and other critical individuals, provide opportunities to learn new skills, and reduce unnecessary risk. From a psychological standpoint, mentors may demonstrate proper work behavior, provide encouragement, discuss advancement and conflict, and provide friendship. Both career and psychosocial attributes, shown in Table 3, will help identify common characteristics of mentor relationships at Toyota (D'Abate et al., 2003; Eby & Allen, 2002; Jenkins, 2013; Kram, 1983).

Table 3
Career and Psychosocial Functions

Career Functions		Psychological Functions	
Sponsorship	The mentor prepares the protégé for becoming a manager, nominates the protégé for desirable projects, and recommends the protégé for both lateral moves and promotions.	*Role modeling*	The protégé imitates work behavior and respects the mentor's attitudes and values. The protégé may wish to obtain a similar position as the mentor. The protégé has respect and admiration for the mentor.
Exposure and visibility	The mentor helps the protégé meet new colleagues, gives assignments to increase contact with critical customers, suppliers, and internal leaders, which may lead to future advancement of the protégé.	*Acceptance and confirmation*	The mentor provides encouragement by showing feelings of respect for the protégé and encourages the protégé to try out new behaviors.
Challenging assignments	The mentor gives tasks and assignments that provide opportunities and tasks so the protégé can learn new skills.	*Counseling*	The mentor and protégé discuss the protégé's competence, advancement, commitment, and relationship conflicts. The mentor shares personal experiences for the protégé to consider as alternatives to problems.
Protecting	The mentor helps to reduce unnecessary risk to the protégé's career advancement and reputation.	*Friendship*	The mentor interacts informally with the protégé during work.
Coaching	A career and/or psychosocial function where the mentor encourages the protégé to advance, shares career history, and provides other means of encouragement.		

Note: Adapted from Kram, K. (1983). Phases of the mentor relationship. *Academy of Management Journal*, 26(4), 608–625. doi.org/10.2307/255910;

Eby, L., & Allen, T. (2002). Further investigation of protégés' negative mentoring experiences. *Group & Organization Management*, 27(4), 456–479. doi.org/10.1177/1059601102238357; and Park, J., Newman, A., Zhang, L., Wu, C., & Hooke, A. (2016). Mentoring functions and turnover intention: The mediating role of perceived organizational support. *The International Journal of Human Resource Management*, 27(11), 1173–1191. doi.org/10.1080/09585192.2015.1062038

Formal and Informal Mentoring

Two types of mentoring may be identified: formal (deliberately paired and structured) and informal (neither deliberate nor structured) (Chun et al., 2012; Rosser, 2005; Srivastava & Jomon, 2013). Informal mentoring is unstructured, usually begins spontaneously, is voluntary, flexible, and often more intimate than formal mentoring (Rosser, 2005). Some studies indicate that informal mentoring is more widespread and also more effective than formal mentoring, though formal mentoring programs have not been well researched, which may skew this understanding (Allen et al., 2006; Rosser, 2005; Srivastava & Jomon, 2013). Formal mentoring programs, though, can only be as successful as the trust established at the onset, because they are not naturally occurring like more informal relationships which begin with some level of trust (Wang et al., 2010).

Characteristics of Mentoring

Both the mentor and the protégé have different roles and responsibilities within the mentoring relationship (Klauss, 1981). Qualifications and characteristics of a good mentor include being an exemplary teacher; possessing strong communication skills; being trustworthy and sensitive to issues of confidentiality; being responsible; showing empathy, openness, and support; and being resourceful (McCann &

Johannessen, 2010). The responsibilities of a mentor often include career strategy advising, acting as a role model, providing individual development plan counseling, giving feedback, providing a vision, and challenging the protégé (Haines, 2003; Klauss, 1981). Protégé responsibilities usually include initiating, sharing, and listening (Klauss, 1981). Mentor relationships include different demographics of age, knowledge, and experience; different types, frequencies, mediums, purposes, and structure of interactions; and degrees of structure and behaviors exhibited. Table 4 identifies different categories, attributes, and options for characterizing attributes. I use these categories in my analysis to help identify characteristics of sensei-protégé relationships at Toyota.

Table 4

Categories, Attributes, and Specific Characteristics of the Mentor-Protégé Relationships

Categories	Attributes	Options for characterizing attributes
Participant demographics	Age	The two parties may be either younger, older, or the same age
	Experience/ knowledge	Either the mentor has more than the learner or it seems not to matter
	Career experience	The two parties may have the same or different backgrounds

Categories	Attributes	Options for characterizing attributes
Interaction characteristics	Duration of the developmental relationship	May be either short-term or long-term
	Regularity of interactions	May be a single event, on a regular schedule, or unscheduled
	Medium	Face-to-face, from a distance, or a combination of the two
	Span	Dyadic, group-oriented, or a combination of the two, with single or multiple mentors
Organizational distance and direction	Direction	Organizational reporting structure may be lateral, downward, or upward. It may come from a different part of the organization's hierarchy
	Location	May be within the organization or an outside relationship
Purpose of interaction	Object of development	May focus on a specific task or a more general area of interest
	Time frame	May focus on short-term performance or long-term development
	Beneficiaries	May benefit one or both parties
Degree of structure	Formality	Either Informal and unstructured or programmatic and formal
	Development coordinator	May include high involvement or may operate on an as needed basis
	Choice to participate	Optional and self-selected or mandatory
	Participant matching	May occur naturally or involve formal matching
	Preparation and support	Preparation and/or support provided is provided
	Interaction termination	May or may not involve formal exit procedures

Categories	Attributes	Options for characterizing attributes
Behaviors exhibited	Learning-related	Collaborating, directing, goal setting, helping on assignments, modeling, observing, problem solving, providing practical feedback, sharing information, and teaching
	Emotional support related	Affirming, Aiding, Befriending, Calming, Confidence building, Counseling, Encouraging, Supporting
	Career progression related	Advocating, Introducing, Sheltering, Socializing

Note. Adapted from D'Abate, C., Eddy, E., & Tannenbaum, S. (2003). What's in a name? A literature-based approach to understanding mentoring, coaching, and other constructs that describe developmental interactions. *Human Resource Development Review*, 2(4), 360–384. doi.org10.1177/1534484303255033

A positive mentoring relationship can lead to important benefits for both the mentor and protégé. From the mentor's standpoint, the potential benefits include increased self-esteem, renewed interest in work, improved status in the organization, and enhanced overall quality of life. Additionally, the process allows the mentor to leave a legacy while at the same time fulfilling his or her own developmental needs (Haines, 2003). From the protégé's standpoint, benefits include increased likelihood of success, job satisfaction, earnings, awareness, and alignment with the organization (Haines, 2003).

Not all mentor-protégé relationships, however, are positive; some result in negative experiences for one or both of the participants (Eby & Allen, 2002). Understanding negative experiences and avoiding the causes of those experiences may help mentors and organizations develop more effective mentor relationships. One study classified negative mentor relationships into five categories: (1) mentor-protégé mismatch, (2) distancing behavior, (3) manipulation, (4) lack of mentor expertise, and (5) general dysfunction; these relationships are described in Table 5 (Eby & Allen, 2002). If a mentee lacks certain skills, does not take feedback seriously, becomes resentful of the mentor, or plays the mentor against other authority figures, the relationship can become unproductive or negative (Haines, 2003). The same can occur if the protégé has unrealistic expectations about advancement, takes part in gossip, or sees the mentor taking credit for their work (Haines, 2003). Additional issues can arise if the mentor lacks time, doesn't keep commitments, or becomes possessive (Haines, 2003). Although outright sabotage or deceit was rare in Eby and Allen's study (2002), the majority of respondents experienced occasions of interpersonal difficulties.

Table 5
Negative Mentoring Experiences, Categories, and Examples

Negative Experiences	Categories and Examples
Mentor-protégé mismatch	General dysfunction
Distancing behavior	Intentional exclusion, neglect, self-absorption
Manipulative behavior	Inappropriate delegation, general abuse of power, taking credit, sabotage, deceit
Lack of mentor experience	Technical incompetence, interpersonal incompetence
General dysfunction	Poor attitude, personal problems

Note. Adapted from Eby, L., & Allen, T. (2002). Further investigation of protégés' negative mentoring experiences. *Group & Organization Management*, 27(4), 456–479. doi.org/10.1177/1059601102238357

Phases of Mentoring

As discussed earlier, the development of mentor-protégé relationships can be broken into four phases: initiation, cultivation, separation, and redefinition (Bullis & Bach, 1989; Kram, 1983). Generally, the initiation phase lasts six to 12 months and the cultivation phase two to five years, with no general timeframe on separation and redefinition (Bullis & Bach, 1989; Kram, 1983). Each phase has a turning point defined by an event associated with a relationship change that increases the sense of belonging and similarity, as shown in Table 6 (Bullis & Bach, 1989). Each phase involves different experiences, functions, and patterns based on individual and organizational circumstances (Kram, 1983). The beginning of the initiation phase and the separation phase are more distinct because they take place at the beginning and end of the relationship. The turning point at which cultivation begins, however, is not easily identified because it may not be a single event (Kram, 1983; Srivastava & Jomon, 2013).

Table 6
Phases, Turning Points, and Characteristics of Mentoring Relationships

Phases	Turning Points	Characteristics
Initiation	Fantasies to concrete expectations Expectations are met Senior manager provides coaching, challenging, visibility Junior manager provides technical assistance, respect, desire Opportunities for interaction around work tasks	Mutual interests defined Task-centered relationship Invitation extended
Cultivation	Both individuals benefit Opportunities for meaningful and more frequent interaction increase Emotional bond deepens	Frequent and meaningful interactions Strong professional and personal relationship Transformative learning occurs Highly productive relationship Mutual growth
Separation	Protégé no longer wants guidance Senior manager can no longer provide support Job rotation, promotion, job change Blocked opportunity may create hostility	Protégé no longer wants guidance Senior manager can no longer provide support Job rotation, promotion, job change Blocked opportunity creates hostility
Redefinition	Stress diminishes, a new relationship formed, gratitude increases Peer status achieved	Peer-like relationship Feelings of mutual gratitude and appreciation

Note: Adapted from Kram, K. (1983). Phases of the mentor relationship. *Academy of Management Journal*, 26(4), 608–625. doi.org/10.2307/255910 and Haines, S. (2003). The Mentor-protégé relationship. *American Journal of Pharmaceutical Education*, 67(82), 458–464.

Initiation Phase

The initiation phase generally begins when the protégé first looks to and receives guidance from a mentor (Kram, 1983). Mentor-protégé relationships may begin in various formal or informal ways (Kram, 1983), although the "turning point" or start of the initiation phase is generally very clear because it is based on when the relationship first begins (Srivastava & Jomon, 2013). The relationship may begin at a hiring interview or with the establishment of a supervisory arrangement, through informal interactions, or through formal or informal decisions of senior leaders to find protégés. Mentor and protégé can be selected entirely by either one of the parties through mutual agreement or be assigned by a coordinator (Sugimoto, 2012).

Cultivation Phase

This phase involves frequent interactions, transformative learning, and the beginning of highly productive work from the protégé (Haines, 2003). As mentioned earlier, the turning point from initiation to cultivation is not always clear (Srivastava & Jomon, 2013) but often involves the protégé's aspirations beginning to become reality as they begin to improve and personalize tasks (Kram, 1983). However, no known empirical study has been conducted investigating turning points from the initiation to the cultivation phases (Srivastava & Jomon, 2013).

Separation Phase

The turning point from the cultivation to the separation phase is usually quite noticeable and often begins with a structural or psychological separation (Viator & Pasewark, 2005). Structural separation can occur when the protégé is hired by a different organization, is transferred to a different geographical location, or changes position in such a way that the mentor relationship ends (Viator & Pasewark, 2005). Typically, when structural or physical separation happens, psychological separation is inevitable (Kram, 1983; Viator & Pasewark, 2005). This phase is marked by the protégé's independence, autonomy, and increasing performance (Viator & Pasewark, 2005). But without physical separation, this phase can potentially lead to jealousy and resentment, as the protégé becomes more independent and, often, a peer to the former mentor (Viator & Pasewark, 2005).

Redefinition Phase

This is a time when the protégé becomes a friend or peer of their previous mentor. The relationship is often redefined so that the mentor and mentee are seen as colleagues, friends, or collaborators, or the relationship may be ended entirely (Kram, 1983; Sugimoto, 2012).

Organizational Benefits of Mentoring

An organization may implement a formal mentoring program to socialize new employees, spread learning, and develop leaders, thereby increasing the speed of organizational development and improving organizational commitment (Chun et al., 2012; Hezlett, 2005; Jenkins, 2013; Singh et al., 2009; Wang et al., 2010). Formal developmental programs advance the protégé's career and increase psychological capital, organizational commitment, workplace wellbeing, and intellectual stimulation, which may result in increased productivity and retention for the organization (Chun et al., 2012; D'Abate et al., 2003; Hezlett, 2005; Klauss, 1981). Protégés believe that organizations with formal mentoring programs value their wellbeing, strongly support their goals and values, take pride in their work accomplishments, and show concern for them (Park et al., 2016). Additionally, mentoring provides a frame of reference to define and solve problems and make decisions. "As members identify with organizations, they learn to adopt the organization's frame of reference and to define problems and issues through that frame ... [and] use organizational premises in their decision making" (Bullis & Bach, 1989, p. 203).

Mentoring in Japanese Culture

Western and Japanese mentoring are different in several ways. Typically, western mentoring relationships are more strategic, structured, and planned, and many times part of the human resource (HR) function within organizations. Japanese mentor relationships, however, traditionally are not part of or facilitated by HR. In the United States mentoring tends to be focused on fast-track promotion and the development of individuals with high talent and potential. Japanese mentors may be called senseis informally, but there seem to be no formal mentoring schemes according to Bright (2005).

Mentoring relationships in Japan are of course impacted by the overall Japanese culture, a culture in which broad-based relationships, the importance of groups, and kinship and other family-type personal relationships are valued. These impacts on relationships have already been discussed in the Japanese management section above and must logically also impact both formal and informal Japanese mentor relationships. Additionally, as an aspect of a vertical society, the culture shows respect for elders and emphasizes their responsibility to help and protect younger individuals. Additionally, career paths are much more predictable in Japan compared to the volatility of careers in the United States (Bright, 2005).

The two types of mentoring relationships within Japan are *senpai-kohai* (senior-junior) characteristic of organizational mentoring, and the *oyabun-kobun* (leader-subordinate) common in apprenticeship relationships. In the senpai-kohai relationship, the senior is, of course, older than the junior; the relationship is mutually beneficial and non-contractual and generally takes place in an organizational context. The relationship is characterized by protection, socialization, human feelings, frankness, benevolent actions, assistance, formality, and relaxation. In the oyabun-kobun relationship, the senior provides guidance and protection and helps find employment for the junior (Bright, 2005).

If the West is to learn from Japanese mentor relationships, the short-term thinking, mistrust, suspicion, and competition characteristic of so much of American society and organizational life must be understood and countered. Typically, in Japan, the senior and the junior member socialize together, creating a relaxed and informal environment where they can discuss personal problems and have frank one-on-one conversations. This trusting relationship is based on the senior providing guidance and favors to the junior, which the junior is informally expected to repay someday. This mutual dependency results in seniors protecting juniors when a failure occurs, since the reputation and status of seniors are also so often associated with the work of their protégés (Bright, 2005).

Summary

This research project explores how leaders who had no previous experience of the Toyota culture and TPS—new hires at Toyota Motor Manufacturing Kentucky—experienced transformation within mentor relationships at Toyota. In order to best characterize these relationships, understanding different types of developmental relationships, which include mentoring both from an American and Japanese standpoint, is necessary. Additionally, understanding characteristics and types of mentoring is necessary in understanding the common characteristics from Toyota Georgetown's relationships.

Mentors or senseis at Toyota were responsible for transferring knowledge in terms of Toyota's production and management systems to the newly hired U.S. workforce. The new developmental relationships between the sensei and the early American leader were almost certainly built on trust from the very beginning, as demonstrated by the success of Toyota at TMMK. Seeing Toyota's plan successfully unfolding in front of them would have provided a powerful model for American executives to learn and adapt TPS. Understanding the key actions that senseis took to move early American leaders through the phases of the mentoring relationship may aid in mentoring and coaching current executives in other organizations and industries in adapting TPS within their organizations. As Gary Convis notes:

> The Japanese have been a critical factor in what we've accomplished at NUMMI. It's not until you work with them, learn the principles from them, that you begin to understand how they see the world and how they feel. My understanding keeps deepening and my commitment to managing in a more open way gets stronger. It has evolved over time from seeing why they do things to how they do them. So, the idea that we could have learned what we have without the Japanese is absurd. (Wilms, 1996, p. 4)

U.S. leaders presumably shifted their mentality from mass production to lean production and the different thinking associated with lean production, giving scholars a critical chance to understand the phases of mentoring. In mass production, buffers of inventory hid uneven work, defects, and problems. Now, in lean production, with work streamlined and with quality control built into the process, team members were expected to call out problems when they actually occurred, and management was responsible for assisting in problem solving. Lower buffers in inventory throughout the assembly line, coupled with Toyota's response to problems, meant that leaders had no choice but to help solve problems to keep the lines running. This shift in process required a shift in leadership styles that Toyota had to teach the newly hired Americans. The phases of mentoring may shed light on how Japanese senseis were able to transition (or not) the thinking of American leaders during the initiation phase into the cultivation phase of the relationship.

At Toyota Georgetown, the decision to use a slow ramp-up schedule and essentially copy the production line from another Toyota plant allowed the Toyota president, Fuji Cho, and others, to begin teaching and coaching TPS, transforming leaders to transform the organization. In addition, the American Toyota manager was paired with a Japanese mentor who remained in Kentucky for several years. These Japanese were charged to

> develop their counterparts only by persuasion—not to do things themselves. This intensely personal approach brought an "eye-opening" moment to most [American Toyota] people. . . . As [Toyota's] plan unfolded during the early years of TMMK, the early American leaders could witness actions and have their Japanese mentors make sense of the context and results. (Mishina & Takeda, 1995, p. 3)

This research aims at understanding the sensei-protégé relationship while focusing primarily on the initiation and cultivation phases of the mentoring relationship so that other firms may more successfully adopt the Toyota Production System.

CHAPTER THREE
METHODOLOGY

The purpose of this study is to learn from the developmental interactions between Japanese senseis and early U.S. leaders at TMMK and specifically to learn why and how these early leaders transitioned from the initiation phase of a mentor relationship to the cultivation phase. I further undertook this study to explore the role this mentoring relationship played in broader organizational change. The objective is to construct a framework for mentors that will serve as a guide in the adaptation of the full array of TPS techniques in other business settings with high levels of leadership. Through the use of qualitative methods, this research aims to identify crucial mentor-protégé interactions so that leaders in other firms and industries can adapt Toyota-style management practices.

Qualitative Research Methods

Following techniques associated with grounded theory, I used semi-structured interviews and oral histories to elicit story driven data for this case study. I then synthesized the data from the semi-structured interview questions and oral histories. Finally, I used interview questions to cull dominant characteristics and interactions of the developmental relationship between the sensei and the early U.S. leaders at TMMK.

Case Study Techniques

Case studies are generally characterized by a bounded system (Merriam & Tisdell, 2016), in this case, the Toyota organization and specifically Toyota Georgetown from 1986 to 1992. In this specific study I focused on the mentoring that took place during the initial phases of TMMK.

Oral History Techniques

The concept of oral history began at Columbia University with the Oral History Research Office in 1948, but the idea has been around for generations in the form of oral tradition and storytelling (Freund, 2009; Ritchie, 2014; Rubel, 2007). This technique involves the researcher establishing a rapport with participants, gathering oral histories and related stories, and establishing a setting for additional semi-structured interviews. The use of this approach for this study elicited specific data regarding mentor relationships and enabled me to perform analyses based on grounded theory techniques.

Oral histories stemming from in depth interviews and characterize a specific qualitative research method. This method placing emphasis on the formation of questions asked to the participant based on some assumptions. In this case, one assumption is that the participants had a sensei help guide them during the early years of TMMK. The qualitative researcher using oral history learns about the experience not only by transactional questions, but also by how the participant lived the particular experience. Oral historians and qualitative researchers seek to understand how someone remembers, values, and orients a memory or experience associated with particular events; in this case, the start of TMMK as it relates to their senseis (Yow, 2014).

Grounded Theory Techniques

According to Glaser and Strauss (2017), grounded theory involves the development of theories from an in-depth analysis of data, which is then used to predict or explain the phenomena under study. Research not grounded in facts and analysis can lead researchers and readers astray, since an ungrounded approach can easily relate data and associated analyses to the researcher's own assumptions and common-sense conjectures. These misapplications do not elicit theoretical perspectives because the process (or lack thereof) is not grounded in participant facts and data. However, within the premises that underlie grounded theory, the process of theory generation is just as important as the theory itself.

Because of a general lack of research addressing turning points from the initiation phase to the cultivation phase in mentoring relationships, coupled with the length of time that passed since the establishment of TMMK, I was unable to use the fullness of a grounded theory approach in this study. Nonetheless, I continuously focused on considerations of grounded theory techniques in constructing the research design and during the analysis.

Narrative Analysis Techniques

Utilizing and interpreting stories in research involves analyzing the structure, elements, and functions of the accounts (Allen, 2017). Narrative analysis used for organizational research may include singular stories or multiple stories from within the organization in combination with a sense of theory making from organizational research literature (Patton, 2014). In this study I used narrative analysis techniques because the stories from within the Toyota organization were gathered and reviewed holistically to begin the theory making process.

Research Design

With the aid of a variety of qualitative research techniques, the research questions aimed to understand the nature and characteristics of the mentor relationships at TMMK and allowed for the emergent understanding of the turning points from the initiation to cultivation phases within the mentor relationships during the early years at TMMK. The overall objective of the research was to establish a theoretical framework for leaders to adopt the Toyota Production System through executive mentoring. I obtained oral histories from participants and categorized the types of developmental interactions between early U.S. leaders at Toyota and their Japanese mentors. I used these to identify actions that helped move protégés from the initiation phase to the cultivation phase within the mentor relationship. Figure 5 below depicts the use of my qualitative data relative for this purpose.

Figure 5
Transition to Cultivation: TMMK 1986–1992

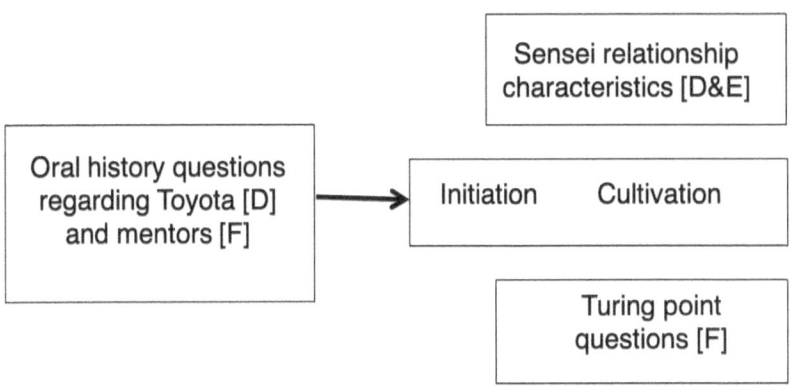

Note. [D] Appendix D: Toyota Oral History-Style Questions; [F] Appendix F: Semi-Structured Interview Questions Regarding Mentors; [E] Appendix E: Sensei Characteristics.

Research Questions

Outcomes associated with the research questions set forth in this study offer a degree of insight to U.S. organizations desiring to adapt and implement TPS-like systems into their organizations outside of the auto industry. As discussed in the objectives and significance of this study, and in conjunction with the literature addressing mentor protégé phases, I arrived at the following two research questions: (a) What are the characteristics of the relationship between early leaders at TMMK and their senseis? (b) What are common themes and steps for early American leaders transitioning from the initiation phase to the cultivation phase of their mentoring relationships? Specifically, the mentor protégé relationship played a large role in successfully implementing TPS with a U.S. workforce. For this reason, I have located the focus of this study on these research questions.

The Interview Process

I conducted face-to-face semi-structured interviews with participants after necessary consent was obtained (see Appendix A, Informed Consent and Invitation for Interviews). To build rapport and capture dependable oral histories, I first asked general questions of the participants, as shown in Appendix B (Oral History-Style Interview Questions), which provided the research with a high degree of flexibility and sequencing (Patton, 2014). On average interviews were about 4 hours and some participants required brief follow-ups. Once responses that related to the mentor relationship were described, I used follow-up questioning to help identify the characteristics and circumstances of those relationships (see Appendix C: Sensei Characteristic Questions; and Appendix D: Semi-Structured Interview Questions).

Obtaining Accurate Oral History

According to Patton (2014), anticipating likely or potential barriers is essential for obtaining accurate oral histories. Older adults are better at telling and making sense of stories than providing verbatim recollections, so being certain that participants understand the research questions and asking open-ended questions both become important techniques in obtaining accurate oral histories. Therefore, to help provide insight into the accuracy of my participants' oral histories, I made a point of noting their mood, emotions, and purposes, while checking for corroboration, refutation errors, or memory lapses. A number of the people interviewed did mentions portions or articles they have been cited in or had written. Participants were encouraged to bring these documents including photographs to the interviews, as they could be used to triangulate and essentially verify stories (Yow, 2014).

Personal memories of actions and thoughts are more precise than memories of the actual timing of events. Thus, those histories told during the semi-structured interviews were categorized as either before or after the "turning point" from initiation into cultivation based on keywords used as described in the methods section. Flashbulb memories of one-time events in the narrator's life are easier to recall than other memories, and, using probes throughout the oral history interviews until flashbulb memories are found, formed a solid foundation for asking more specific questions about these relationships. These flashbulb memories could also indicate a turning point in the mentor relationship and are flagged as such (Yow, 2014).

Participants and Sampling

Participants included individuals hired in leadership positions at TMMK between 1985 and 1992. These individuals had to be willing to voluntarily participate and be able to do so with informed consent. Rodger Lewis, a key informant and potential participant, sent a participation letter, approved by the IRB, to other potential participants. Then I employed linear snowball sampling to select further participants for both the oral histories and the semi-structured interview questions. Rodger Lewis snowballed to Russ Scaffede to Catesby Prewitt to David Meier, and David Meier to Jeff Merriss, Bob Wilson, and John Allen. The names and positions during their time at Georgetown, as agreed to during the process of obtaining consent, as well as the dates of their interviews, are shown in Table 7 below. Given the availability of individuals that meet the criteria and the time commitment necessary to complete this study I believe these seven individuals are the best first step in understanding the sensei-protégé relationship for this case study.

Table 7

Names, Roles, and Interview Dates of Participants

Participant	First Position	Second Position	Date and Setting
Rodger Lewis	Assistant Manager of Quality (Manufacturing)	Manager of Quality (Power Train)	October 2018 In-person
Russ Scaffede	General Manager of Power Train	Vice President of Power Train	October 2019 In-person
Catesby Prewitt	Team Leader Manufacturing	Manager Maintenance Power Train	December 2019 In-person
David Meier	Team Leader Manufacturing	n/a	January 2019 In-person
Jeff Merriss	Team Member Manufacturing	Junior Engineer Manufacturing	January 2019 In-person

Participant	First Position	Second Position	Date and Setting
John Allen	Human Resources	n/a	January 2019 In-person
Bob Wilson	Team Member	Lean Leader at Toyota Supplier	January 2019 Skype

Setting

Interviews were conducted at a time and location amenable to the participants, typically in a neutral area such as a hotel conference room in a city located near the participants' residences. All interviews were conducted face-to-face, except that with Robert Wilson, which was conducted via Skype, because he lives in Texas and travel was not feasible given budget and time constraints. I used the physical and virtual meetings not only to collect information but also to establish rapport and trust, which further increased the credibility of the data collected.

Instruments

Oral histories, archival data (if available), and qualitative data specific to the semi-structured interview questions were collected during this research project. The oral history interview questions were used to start the interview (see Appendix D: Toyota Oral History-Style Questions). At a time that I discerned was comfortable for both the narrator and myself, the interview moved to the specific questions in Appendix E (Sensei Characteristic Questions) and

Appendix F (Semi-Structured Interview Questions Regarding Mentors). Some of the questions contained in Appendix F were copied with permission from the mentor research conducted by Alisic et al. (2016).

Informed Consent and Final Release

The recruitment letter contained in Appendix A and the consent form contained in Appendix B were used to recruit potential participants and obtain consent. Appendix C (Deed of Gift) was signed by the participants after the delivery of the draft manuscript and video documentary.

Data Analysis

I analyzed the data from each set of semi-structured interviews separately and processed the analyses into the final presentations with the oral histories. As Table 8 demonstrates, I used a combination of closed and open questions with probes to determine demographics, perceptions of knowledge, positive/negative and emotional experiences. While analyzing data of positive/negative experiences I found many experiences coded as negative involved emotion, and actually involved a positive experience. Therefore, I explored this phenomenon using keywords linked to emotion, described in that section. To analyze the initiation to cultivation transformation, I categorized the stories of the sensei relationship into the four phases of the mentor relationship (initiation, cultivation, separation, and redefinition) based on keywords and their meanings noted in a later section, found in Kram (1983) within the initiation and cultivation phases. Within those stories, I explored potential turning points from initiation to cultivation to further understand the transformation happening within the mentor relationship.

Table 8
Data Analysis Methods

RQ1	Type of Questions	Data Analysis Methods
Demographics; Schedule of Events	Closed Questions	Descriptive Findings
Perception of Knowledge	Closed questions with open probes	Narrative Analysis, Grounded Theory Techniques, and Oral History Technique
Positive/Negative and Emotional Experiences	Closed questions with probes and open questions	Narrative Analysis, Grounded Theory Techniques, and Oral History Techniques
RQ2		
Mentoring Process	Open questions	Grounded Theory Techniques and Oral History Techniques

Sensei-Protégé Characteristics

The first interview question I asked a participant was: What are the characteristics of the developmental relationship between early leaders at TMMK and their Japanese counterparts? This question aimed to identify the most prominent relationship characteristics, including demographics, perceptions of knowledge, schedule of interactions, positive/negative experiences, and degree of trust (D'Abate et al., 2003) in each mentoring relationship.

The worksheet and semi-structured interview questions related to sensei characteristics (Appendix B) were analyzed to check for similarities and differences among participants. Based on conversations revolving around Appendix C, Sensei Characteristic Questions, I determined the characteristics and structures of the relationship. Such analysis included both common and unique responses to determine dominant characteristics of the mentor relationship between the sensei and the early American leader, which I used to characterize that relationship.

Demographic and Other Characteristics

The group of questions related to demographics, schedule, and degree of trust were asked and answered using closed questions; therefore, these findings are descriptive. Characteristics related to the perception of knowledge were asked using a closed question; however, the answers were elaborated upon and the question was in general interpreted or best answered by an open question. Therefore, narrative analysis was used to interpret the elements of these answers and the stories within the answers to draw conclusions.

Other characteristics including reporting structure and nature of the mentor relationship were asked via both closed and open questions. For those who held only one position at Toyota, I treated the findings descriptively. However, some participants held multiple roles within Toyota during their tenure. Consequently, their answers were multifaceted and I used narrative analysis to better understand the nature of the mentor relationships.

Emotional Behaviors and Negative Experiences

Narrative analysis, grounded theory techniques, and oral history techniques were used to analyze negative emotional experiences. Narrative analysis using open questions was used regarding negative experiences. Grounded theory was used by searching code words regarding negative experiences that may have been brought up during other, unanticipated, parts of the interview. Oral history techniques, specifically probing, were used to gather further information about potential negative experiences once the participant brought them to light. Additionally, grounded theory techniques were used to categorize negative experiences into types of negative experiences, which were analyzed.

Emotional experiences and behaviors were uniquely analyzed using keywords describing negative mentor experiences from Eby and Allen (2002) in the transcripts, as well as specific prompts. This involved the use of grounded theory techniques by establishing categories based on keywords, again taken from Eby and Allen (2002). I used them to search for negative experiences. They included the following terms: *negative, weak, deny, reject, oppose, mismatched, resist, exclude, neglect, absorption, inappropriate, abuse, credit-taking, sabotage, deceit, incompetent,* and *bad.* To explore emotions in more detail, I searched for the following emotions based on a list developed from Ortony and Turner (1990) regarding basic emotions and keywords: *anger, aversion, courage, dejection, desire, despair, fear, hate, hope, love, sadness, disgust, joy, surprise, happiness, interest, wonder, sorrow, rage, terror, anxiety, contempt, distress, guilt, shame, grief, elation, subjection, tender, pain, pleasure, expectancy, panic, acceptance,* and *anticipation.*

Stories about negative mentor relationships from previous employers were not taken into consideration. Other stories that included keywords outside of an emotional context were also removed. An example of this would be the search for the word *weak* when that word appeared in a discussion of a *weak* point in the machinery.

From Initiation to Cultivation

Research Question Two asks: What are common steps for early American leaders transitioning from the initiation phase to the cultivation phase of the mentoring relationship? Again, using grounded theory techniques, transcripts were analyzed using keywords. The first two categories include words related to the initiation and cultivation phases based on characteristics and turning points. Keywords for Initiation, derived from Kram (1983) and Haines (2003) included *initiation, watch, teach, show, demonstrate, assist, complete, listen, assign, perform, attend, guide, protect, associate, oversee, supervise, coach,* and *challenge*. Keywords for Cultivation included *understand, grasp, change, improve, grow, enhance, promote, expand, transform, appreciate, comprehend, reveal, assimilate, incorporate, embody, integrate,* and *embrace*. These two sets of keywords allowed the researcher to separate task-centered stories characteristic of the initiation phase from stories of transformative learning characteristic of the cultivation phase. Once all the data were coded, results were analyzed to separate experiences into initiation and cultivation phases, with potential turning points. A summary of how these keywords were used to segment the data is shown in Table 9.

Table 9
Key Words for Separating Experience

Initiation	Turning Point	Cultivation
Relationship centered on tasks	More opportunities for meaningful interactions benefiting both individuals and the organization	Transformative learning occurs
Interaction around work tasks		Frequent and meaningful interactions
Technical assistance from protégé		Mutual growth
Key Words: watch, teach show, demonstrate, assist, complete, listen, assign, perform, attend, guide, protect, associate, oversee, supervise, coach, challenge		Key Words: understand, grasp, change, improve, grow, enhance, promote, expand, transform, appreciate, comprehend, reveal, assimilate, incorporate, embody, integrate, embrace

I noted the parts of the narratives that showed both the mentor and the mentee benefiting from the relationship and that indicated meaningful interactions between the individuals and the organization as potential turning points. Additionally, each statement addressing the sensei was coded as a potential turning point, and the proceeding interactions were analyzed. Although this is not a full grounded theory study, these techniques, grounded in facts and intended for analysis, helped legitimize the final product. For example, the theme of protection was discovered by using a grounded theory methodology: I identified negative experiences from key words, discovered that these experiences coded as negative were actually positive, and further exploring the data until I discovered the theme of protection. This approach will assist leaders in other businesses and industry sectors to learn from these experiences and to internalize the TPS techniques (Glaser & Strauss, 2017; Merriam & Tisdell, 2016).

Mentoring Perspective

A holistic analysis of the mentoring process itself was the most complicated. Transcripts from John Allen, who had the Human Resources perspective of the mentoring process, seemed to show the most background knowledge related to the questions. Therefore, I used his transcript as the basis of the analysis and to lay the foundation for understanding the mentoring process. Narrative analysis and grounded theory were used to link stories from other participants to John's explanation of the overall process. The grounded theory approach of categorizing key words closely matched John's step-by-step analysis of the early mentor-mentee relationships for the first U.S. leaders involved with TMMK.

Considerations

This study posed minimal risk due to the nature of the questions, but legal and accuracy risks were possible. The subjects were being interviewed for their experiences in a business success from over 30 years ago, and their stories were generally not highly sensitive. Nevertheless, the subjects were a small and identifiable group of people whose real names were used. Below I discuss these ethical risks in addition to matters of credibility and other considerations.

Ethical Risks

The risk existed that participants might, in the course of telling their stories, disclose information about activities or events that could prove embarrassing, controversial, or illegal. To protect the participants, I flagged such information for discussion with that interviewee and jointly discerned the best way forward. I also allowed each participant to carry out member checks of a rough draft of the manuscript and documentary before publishing and signing off for release. I redacted the real names of those who were not participating in the study and used pseudonyms unless permission was obtained. I carefully secured the records of the interviews, transcripts, and any other archival data obtained and only shared this information via password-protected links to those involved in transcribing. Approval for this study was obtained in advance from the Indiana University of Pennsylvania's Institutional Review Board (IRB).

Credibility and Trustworthiness

Participants primarily ranged from being retired, current entrepreneurs, or consultants. None of the participants were current employees of Toyota, nor seemed to have any desire to be an employee of Toyota in the future, given age and other responsibilities. Therefore, there seemed to be little or no holding back or falsification of statements.

Additionally, and coincidently, no participant was an employee of Toyota's competitors or any other organization besides the ones they owned themselves or were consulting for on a limited basis. Many stories seemed to overlap and no significant contradictions emerged, which added to the credibility of both the participants and the results.

Confidentiality, Anonymity, and Privacy

Confidentiality in this study primarily entails protecting the data during the research process until all parties have signed the Deed of Gift. This research offered confidentiality or anonymity if the participant wanted to redact certain names or stories prior to publication.

Results were synthesized with the oral histories to create a draft manuscript and documentary, which were approved as a draft by participants using Appendix E (Final Release Form). I kept the approved transcripts and supporting documents, which may be used for future research and publication. Once the dissertation is approved, I will create a presentation and implementation plan based on transferrable knowledge to help create and improve existing mentor and executive education programs in the adoption of TPS. The completed manuscript, supplemented by additional research, will be used as the basis of a book or as an article for an academic journal.

Summary

This qualitative research study employed techniques from case study research, grounded theory, narrative analysis, and oral histories to answer research questions regarding the characteristics of the mentor relationship between senseis and early U.S. leaders at TMMK. The study documents the TMMK processes addressing the mentor relationship from initiation to cultivation. Participants included leaders employed by TMMK from 1986 to 1992 and were selected using snowball sampling until the researcher had enough information to re-focus the data gathering tools and interview questions. Participants were interviewed face-to-face or, in one case via Skype, in an oral history style interview with the aid of semi-structured questions. Data were analyzed to determine common characteristics and interactions that shed light on possible turning points to give the researcher an understanding of how the mentor relationship is transferrable to other businesses considering the adaption of TPS.

CHAPTER FOUR
RESULTS

This study involved investigating the developmental interactions between Japanese senseis (mentors) and early U.S. leaders at Toyota Motor Manufacturing Kentucky (TMMK). Specifically, the research investigated why and how these early U.S. leaders transitioned from the initiation phase at the start of the mentor relationship to the active and transformational participation characteristic of the cultivation phase and the role this mentoring relationship played in broader organizational change. This research involved the use of qualitative methods for data collection and analysis as outlined previously.

In this chapter I will present results from my analysis of the data. I will first discuss the characteristics of the structured formal relationships that existed during the first three years of the Toyota Georgetown operation. Then, I will discuss what this research has shown to be the mentoring process from initiation to cultivation at TMMK. Although Bright (2005) has identified protection as one of many terms associated with the senpai-kohai relationship, perhaps the most striking finding of this research is the extent to which protection was central to the mentoring relationships in the early days at Toyota Georgetown. As previously discussed, protection can take many forms: a mentor may provide protection as a father figure, provide protection by reducing unnecessary risks to advancement and reputation, or provide protection by taking on the responsibility of helping younger individuals (Bright, 2005; Eby & Allen, 2002; Klauss, 1981; Kram, 1983; Park et al., 2016).

Study Participants

This study involved interviews with seven participants, some of whom had multiple sensei relationships at Toyota. The data collection yielded over 24 hours of video and audio and over a hundred stories. Six of the seven interviews were conducted face-to-face, and one was conducted via Skype. Some other prospective participants were not able to participate due to the length of time required for the interview and, therefore, further research is needed to better explore the initial findings of this dissertation. Participants and their place in the organization are listed below, noting that the titles are not necessarily the exact titles used by Toyota.

> Participant 1: Manager, Rodger Lewis
> Participant 2: General Manager, Russ Scaffede
> Participant 3: Group Leader, Manager, Catesby Prewitt
> Participant 4: Group Leader, David Meier
> Participant 5: Manager (without a dedicated Executive Coordinator), John Allen
> Participant 6: Team Leader, Jeff Merriss
> Participant 7: External Leader (for Toyota's Suppliers), Bob Wilson

Figure 6 below demonstrates the initial mentoring structure at Toyota's operations in Georgetown, Kentucky. Essentially, the senior executive coordinator, a Toyota Japanese leader, reported directly to Fujio Cho, the president of Toyota Georgetown. A group of Japanese Executive Coordinators, all seasoned Toyota leaders, reported to the Senior Executive Coordinator. The executive coordinators were responsible for mentoring the American managers and the general manager. The coordinators, sometimes referred to as trainers, reported to the executive coordinators and were responsible for mentoring group leaders. Figures 7 and 8 show how some relationships at Toyota were informal between a team leader and an executive coordinator. Other relationships took place outside of Toyota, typically at a Toyota supplier company, using a former Toyota executive as a consultant and an American leader as the employee that worked closely with the consultant.

Figure 6

Structure of Formal Mentoring at Toyota

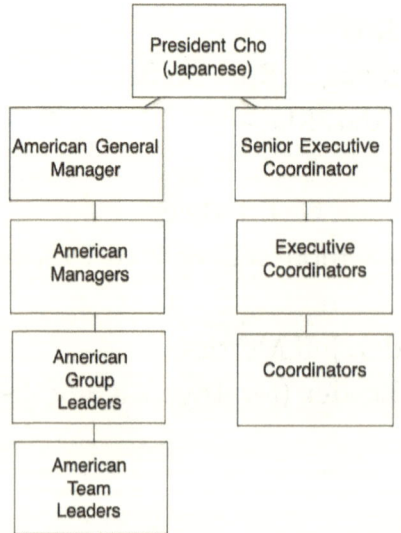

Figure 7
Structure of Informal Mentoring at Toyota

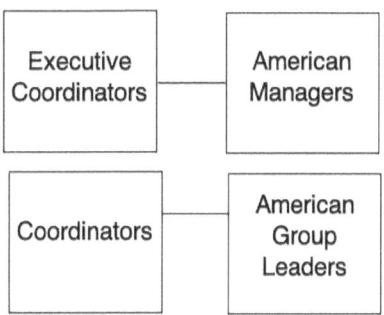

Figure 8
Formal Mentoring at Toyota's Suppliers

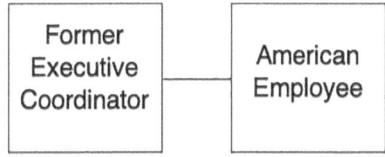

Early Mandatory Developmental Relationships

This section covers organizational structure and participant roles, which help define the different characteristics of the TMMK mentor relationships both early on and in later years. Generally, what participants described in this section included both upper level managers (i.e., managers and general managers) and middle levels of management (i.e., group leaders). Team leaders (frontline supervisors) and team members may have had informal relationships but generally did not have a formal dedicated sensei specifically assigned to them. Although both informal and formal; relationships are important and discussed, the focus in this section is on mandatory relationships, which seemed to intentionally pair top-notch senseis with newly hired group leaders and managers—a critical group in the long-term success of Toyota.

The section on relationship characteristics summarizes demographics, age, interactions, formality, and purpose and timeframe of the relationship. These characteristics helped identify differences in the structure between group leaders and managers and between their respective senseis. These early mandatory developmental relationships seemed to be built into the organizational structure of Toyota, Georgetown. Therefore, understanding the organizational structure at the time is essential in understanding and the types and purpose of sensei-protégé relationships relative to successfully adopting a TPS type environment. Though I cover both managers and group leaders in this section, there seemed to be a higher degree of structure with the relationships established at the group leader level, which I discuss more specifically in a later section about the mentoring process.

Organizational Structure and Participant Roles

The first research question asked: What are the characteristics of the developmental relationship between early leaders at TMMK and their Japanese counterparts? This question aimed to identify the most prominent characteristics of these relationships, including the demographics, behaviors, perceptions of knowledge, frequency of interactions, positive/negative experiences, and degree of trust (D'Abate et al., 2003) and focuses on the relationships that fall into the category described in Figures 6 and 7. The majority of the data used in this study were obtained by analyzing the responses to the interview questions contained in Appendix D.

The results indicate that as Toyota began collaboration with the American workforce in Georgetown, Kentucky, it took a structured approach to utilizing Japanese senseis as executive coordinators and coordinators. All Japanese coordinators reported to a senior Japanese executive coordinator, who ultimately reported to Fujio Cho, the Japanese president of TMMK. The general manager had a dedicated executive coordinator, and he (the general manager) reported directly to Mr. Cho. These relationships were mandatory. Within the established structure, the coordinators were dedicated to a specific person or group on recurring cycles. A cycle consisted of three years for executive coordinators working with managers and three months for coordinators working with group leaders.

Data from the interviews suggests that American mentees had an overall more positive experience during the first three years of Toyota Georgetown compared to the experiences they had over the next three years. One participant explicitly stated that the first group of senseis was Toyota's "cream of the crop" because this initiative in Kentucky was of the upmost importance in Japan. This downplayed later cycles and therefore the characteristics discussed below include only the initial three-year mandatory relationships. Figure 9 shows the different types of relationships the participants in the study developed at Toyota. As shown in Figure 9, the relationships can be further categorized as:

1. Direct Reporting: The American general man-

ager reported directly to the Japanese President, which is a unique case that only pertains to Russ Scaffede and Fujio Cho.
2. Dedicated manager: Japanese executive coordinators mentored American general managers, managers, and assistant managers. This pertains to Rodger Lewis, Russ Scaffede, and Catesby Prewitt (Catesby's second relationship at Toyota).
3. Dedicated group leader: The relationship between a group-leader (a supervisor, the lowest level salaried American, located below the managers on the organization structure) and a Japanese coordinator/trainer.

The word "dedicated" is used because many participants noted interactions with multiple senseis or had an ad-hoc or informal relationship with an executive coordinator. This is particularly relevant for David Meier and Catesby Prewitt and their coordinators.

Figure 9

Reporting and Mentoring Relationships at TMMK

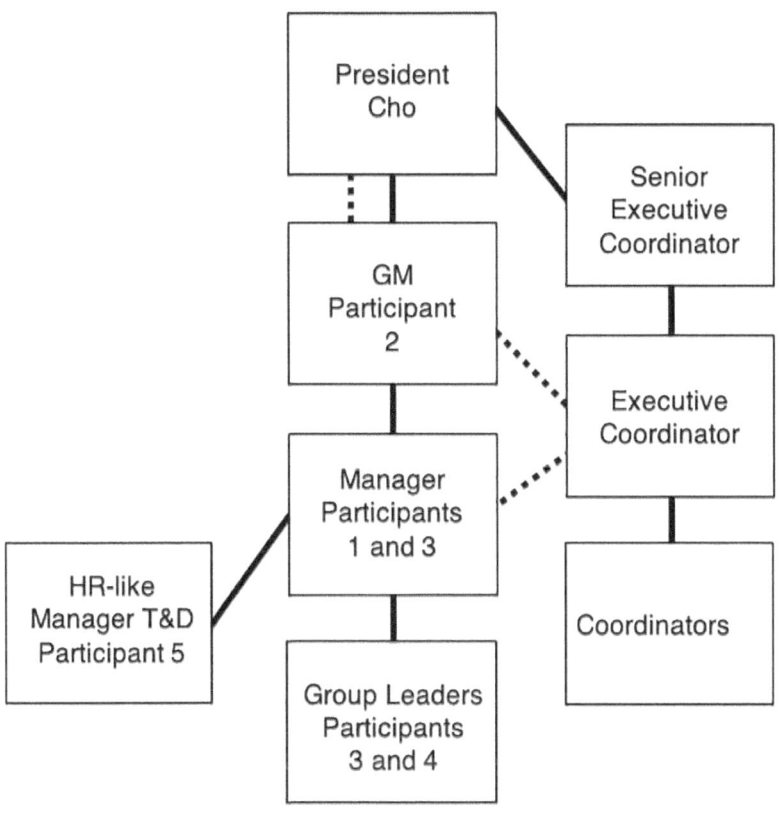

Note. Reporting Relationships ―――――
Dedicated Mentoring Relationships ··················

Characteristics of the Mentor Relationships at Toyota

The sources of the data on the common characteristics of these relationships are the mandatory ones with coordinators and executive coordinators, which in this study involved participants one through four listed above. Participant two, the general manager, who was promoted to vice president, said that Mr. Cho, the President of Toyota Georgetown, was his primary mentor.

Participant three, Catesby Prewitt, was a group leader who was promoted to manager and who had an overall positive experience with his sensei during the first three-year cycle but an overwhelmingly negative experience with his sensei during the second three-year iteration. This negative experience, because it did not take place during the first cycle, is not included in this data. Participant five listed above was a manager in the Human Resources group but did not have a dedicated relationship to an executive coordinator and was therefore left out of this discussion. His interview is explored later and provided the most insight into the process of initiation. Relationships that were not formal sensei-protégé relationships within Toyota were also excluded. This enabled me to analyze the positive sensei-protégé relationships during the first cycle.

Age and Gender of Participants

All participants and all senseis discussed were male. The ages of the Japanese senseis were about the same or older than their American counterparts. Regarding gender, participants noted that all relationships were male-male, and none were aware of any Japanese-American opposite gender relationships. Age is important, because as one participant noted, some senseis may have worked many years to get to the group leader level in Japan and that Toyota was hiring new (and presumably younger) people for Georgetown. The majority of executive coordinators were about the same age as their manager counterparts, presumably because they had been in the auto-industry for about the same length of time.

Perception of Knowledge/Experience

The participants generally acknowledged that their mentors had more knowledge about TPS and in some cases more technical knowledge than they did. All agreed that the Japanese had less knowledge than they did about how to work with an American workforce.

Technical knowledge varied according to a participant's background; the managers interviewed came from Volkswagen and General Motors and had considerable technical knowledge on how to build a car, whereas group leaders had less perceived technical knowledge than their senseis. In the case of a maintenance manager, he noted that he might have had more specific knowledge of the actual equipment.

Duration, Purpose, and Timeframe

The duration of the developmental relationship (short-term or long-term); purpose of interaction (general or specific); and timeframe/purpose of interaction (short-term performance or long-term development) have been combined into this one section, given the nature of the answers provided by participants. Answers to the duration question helped shape the understanding of the three-year and three-month cycles of executive coordinators and coordinators as previously discussed. The purpose of interactions was more general at the manager level and revolved around understanding TPS and more specific at the group leader level and involved the establishment of a daily regimen, including leading the daily morning meeting. In the words of a group-leader participant: "We had to learn leadership, we had to learn TPS, we had to learn the processes and operations, so there was like three things going on there that we had to do, and we had to do it fast."

Answers to the timeframe/purpose of interaction questions were quite diverse and included both a short-term and a long-term focus, a short-term focus with long-term outcomes, and long-term development.

Schedule of Interactions, Organizational Distance, Direction, and Span

All participants noted that the regularity of interactions with their mentor varied from a one-time-only event to regularly scheduled interactions to those that were unscheduled. The span of interaction options given to participants included dyadic (just the two of us), group-centered, and interactions involving several senseis. In all cases the participants noted that the medium of mentoring interaction took place face-to-face.

Though all the participants had a dedicated executive coordinator, they also acknowledged interactions with many other senseis that were dedicated to other individuals and groups. Although some interactions were in a group setting, most were dyadic, including some that were with a non-dedicated Japanese coordinator. Consequently, the organizational distance/direction answers helped shape Figures 4 and 5 as previously discussed. One participant indicated that he and his coordinator were essentially on the same organizational level. The general manager noted that his primary mentor was Mr. Cho, the president of Toyota Georgetown, which was a higher position than his. Managers interacted with coordinators as well. The HR manager noted that his executive coordinator sat higher on the organization chart and spent more time with his American boss than with him, which was part of my decision to categorize this as a non-dedicated mentor relationship.

Location

All four participants included in these characteristics noted that the location of these interactions were internal because everyone was a Toyota employee. One participant had a relationship with a sensei outside Georgetown, as that person moved from Toyota to a board member/consultant role at a Toyota supplier. This American was hired to be the internal TPS leader and was mentored by a former Toyota Japanese executive.

Structure, Initiation, and Matching

Participants noted that the degree of structure within the actual mentor-protégé interactions was perceived as informal and unstructured, although the choice to participate was mandatory—the sensei was chosen by Toyota and was formally matched to the mentee. Therefore, these relationships may best be described as formal and structured with informal and unstructured interactions.

Developmental Coordinator, Support, and Preparation

In the semi-structured interviews, one question asked about the involvement of the "developmental coordinator," which implied an HR-type function coordinating the relationship. Participants tended to misunderstand this question, presumably because the concept of a developmental coordinator was foreign to sensei-protégé relationships. This provides evidence that coordinating the sensei-protégé relationship was not a specific HR function at Toyota, as it is in many U.S. companies discussed in the literature review chapter. Additionally, as noted, all of the senseis reported to a Senior Executive Coordinator, who reported directly to Mr. Cho.

Trustworthiness of Senseis and Toyota

All but one participant strongly agreed with the statements that both Toyota and their senseis were trustworthy. One participant agreed that both were trustworthy, but the question proved to be difficult to answer due to apparent discrepancies in trust between the Americans themselves. In other words, the participant seemed to distrust one or some Americans that were Toyota employees and therefore could not state that Toyota was trustworthy.

Separation and Redefinition

All participants noted that their relationships with their Japanese mentors ended as planned. The one exception was that of the general manager, who left Toyota after five years to pursue another opportunity, thus ending his relationship with Mr. Cho. Everyone who expressed having an overall positive experience with their dedicated mentors noted that if the relationship continued it gradually transitioned to that of a colleague, to a friend, and finally to a collaborator.

Summary of Early Mandatory Developmental Relationships

The organizational structure for early mandatory developmental relationships included coordinators as senseis for group leaders and executive coordinators as senseis for managers, all of whom ultimately reported to Fujio Cho, the president. Generally, for early mandatory developmental relationships, most senseis were the same age or older than their American charges. In terms of perceptions of knowledge, senseis were noted as knowing more about TPS, the American leaders knew more about the American workforce. Technical knowledge, however, varied. Managers seemed to have three-year relationships with their senseis, whereas group leaders may have had shorter cycles. Participation in the relationships was mandatory, but as discussed, informal relationships began to emerge. 11 10 shows a summary of these results.

Table 10

Characteristics of Early Mandatory Relationships

Characteristic/ Demographic	Manager	Group Leader
Age of Sensei	Same Age or Older	Older
Timeframe of Relationship	3-year relationship	3-month rotating
Position of Sensei	Executive Coordinator	Coordinator
Participation	Mandatory	Mandatory

Mentoring and Protection

The major finding regarding emotional experiences is that *protection* seems to be a common theme in successful sensei-protégé relationships. Protection is defined in Chapter 2 as when "the mentor helps to reduce unnecessary risk to the protégé's career advancement and reputation." I uncovered this theme, first, by exploring negative experiences. Negative experiences were coded from keywords including *negative, weak, deny, reject, oppose, mismatched, resist, exclude, neglect, absorption, inappropriate, abuse, credit-taking, sabotage, deceit, incompetent,* and *bad*. I organized these experiences into three categories: negative experience, neutral experience, and positive experience. Coincidently, many seemingly negative stories had positive endings, and many of these stories seemed to have the theme of the sensei protecting the protégé; often occurring during an emotionally charged experience. So, I explored this phenomenon further.

Expanding upon just the experiences that were found using negative keywords, I then searched all transcripts for additional emotional experiences. I used the following keywords from Ortony and Turner (1990): emotion, anger, aversion, courage, dejection, desire, despair, fear, hate, hope, love, sadness, disgust, joy, surprise, happiness, interest, wonder, sorrow, rage, terror, anxiety, contempt, distress, guilt, shame, grief, elation, subjection, tender, pain, pleasure, expectancy, panic, acceptance, and anticipation. The methods employed in exploring emotional experiences yielded many stories. Stories involving emotions were categorized into six groups: (1) family/hobbies/interests; (2)

initiation; (3) cultivation; (4) separation; (5) redefinition (6) other non-Toyota relationships; and (7) other. Of these groups, I analyzed initiation and cultivation and found additional stories that demonstrated protection.

Stories of Protection

For the first generation of Japanese coordinators, many negative events weren't between the actual dedicated Japanese sensei and the American protégé. Rather, the sensei stepped in and protected the protégé from a potentially negative or emotional situation involving other Japanese coordinators or trainers.

These stories include Americans becoming frustrated because of perceived Japanese lack of emotion (story one), but also American managers protecting the workforce from those occasions when the Japanese failed to control their emotions (story two). In story three, a protégé became frustrated and a mentor protected him from getting into a more difficult emotional situation by removing him from the situation. In story four, one Japanese coordinator was yelling at an American after a misunderstanding, only to be immediately corrected by the American's sensei. In story five, the Japanese sensei protected the American from inadvertent negative perceptions of the workforce when he appeared to be favoring certain team members. Similarly, in story six, Mr. Cho protected an American from being labeled as the leader of a program versus the leader of TPS, which was essential for the success of both Toyota and the manager. In story seven, the sensei protected the protégé by preparing him for an emotionally charged conversation by coaching him to provide an appropriate answer. In stories eight and nine, senseis protected protégés from the negative consequences of failure. The nine stories are detailed as follows.

Story Number One: Americans Experience Frustration

Cultural differences and the Japanese insistence on facts were sometimes a source of frustration for the Americans.

> I was amazed at their patience and perseverance. Earlier on we would be in meetings and the American staff would be pointing fingers, or we would be in our own group venting and just wanting them to agree with us on "the other guy is wrong," you know, [but] they wouldn't do it. They would continue to come back saying, "What about this, what about this?" and you know, it was very frustrating to us that they were so patient.

Story Number Two: American Leader Protecting the Workforce

This story exhibits a type of reverse-protection—an American calming the Japanese coordinator.

> The first cars we built; they were inspected at the end. It was a Friday, and we inspected this group of cars, and we were gonna marshal them, and some of us Americans just thought about it. "Gee, there might be some defects on these cars, let's go check them on Saturday." So, a group of us come in on Saturday and we checked all the cars, made sure there was absolutely nothing on them, and we actually confirmed them to be shipped.

What we did not know was that our Japanese counterparts had come in after we left, and put some new defects on the cars to see if we could find them in the final inspection process. We did not know that, and so we released the cars early, so when we came in on Monday morning, well, the cars were gone and he wanted to know where the cars were at, we told them we released them.

Well [my executive coordinator] is probably every bit of 5 feet 4 and he was probably jumping 8 to 10 feet high in the air and wanted to know where the cars were at. Then finally . . . I said, "Why?" And he said, "We make defects, we make defects!" And then I realized what he had done because they wanted to see if we would find the new defects.

It was a PDCA [plan-do-check-act], and I was calming him cause we're right in the middle of the plant and he's jumping up and down, everybody wanted to know why he has started jumping up and down. And I was probably gonna tell them it was his magnets in his shoes sticking to the floor, 'cause you know what Japanese believe in—they use magnets in their beds and they use it in the soles of their shoe 'cause they believe there's positive energy. I kept telling people, "It's probably his magnets in his shoes or something, that's causing him to jump up," but we had to calm them sometimes 'cause they would get emotional, you know.

This story shows that in extreme cases even the best first-generation executive coordinators would sometimes become emotional. Shipping defects in the first batch of cars built in North America could have turned into a major quality and public relations nightmare for Toyota. Therefore, in this extremely tense case, the sensei was not able to control his emotions. The mentee, though, with more information, used protection in trying to calm his sensei down and explain his behavior to other Americans. It is important to note that the cars were found and corrected before any customer received them.

Story Number Three: Frustration of American Worker
In this story, the mentor stepped in and protected the protégé from a potentially negative situation with a Japanese trainer. The American group leader described the situation as follows:

> I couldn't understand, I couldn't keep track of what he was saying, and I panicked, and I said, "No, no, no, no stop!" ... But I remember he [his assigned Japanese coordinator] came over and ... said [to him], "Let's go get a cup coffee." We took off; we went and got a cup of coffee. So, they [someone else, probably another Japanese] must've said something to him that "Your guy [the American] is acting up or nervous, or something."

By removing his mentee from the situation, the sensei protected him from further conflict with the Japanese trainer.

Story Number Four: Mentee Stopped Production
In this story, the American's sensei actually corrects the behavior of another Japanese as follows. From a quality standpoint, Rodger Lewis had responsibilities involving every process at Toyota, including stamping, body shop, paint shop, assembly, final assembly, chassis, and shipping. Because he couldn't be everywhere at the same time, and knowing that paint is a significant point in the process where quality is difficult to re-work, he instructed his group leader in the body shop (just before painting) to not release any vehicles until he was able to inspect them. Shortly thereafter, Rodger had a negative experience with another sensei. During this negative interaction, Rodger's sensei protected Rodger from the other sensei's negative reactions. In Rodger's words:

> [All of a sudden] the Executive Coordinator who was a sensei in the body shop was screaming. "You, why you, why you stop production, why you don't come see, why you don't come see?" And he was very excited and animated about it, and he was screaming a little bit and [then] . . . I saw my sensei walk up behind me and get a hold of the other sensei and tell him his behavior was very bad, that he should not have exhibited that in front of team members.

Story Number Five: Protection from Inadvertent Neglect of Team Members
Rodger describes how he walked the floor every day, taking the same route. Consequently, he stopped each day with the same team during their break. His sensei pointed

out the unintended consequences of walking the same route each day by saying, "You stop every day and take break with team members." To which Rodger replied that he felt that it was a good thing he stopped and talked with team members.

His sensei responded: "No, bad, you always stop in the same area. Why don't you stop with other team members, other team members think maybe you don't like them." Rodger's sensei was thus able to provide him simple and fast coaching to change his behavior, which may have led to unintended consequences and less mutual trust and respect between him and the American workforce.

Story Number Six: Introduction of Total Preventative Maintenance (TPM)

Russ Scaffede, the first General Manager and later Vice President of Toyota's powertrain division, described his passion for implementing long-term total preventative maintenance but was blocked by Director Hayakawa, head of the entire powertrain division.

> Well, the next thing I know I've been asked that I go see Mr. Cho. So, I go to Mr. Cho and he says, "I hear you want to implement TPM in the powertrain?"
>
> And I said, "I really do, Mr. Cho. You guys are trained in everything, but I don't understand it. You're not training preventative maintenance."
>
> Mr. Cho said, "Well, what I'm going to do is I'm going to send you to Japan for a week, but your job when you come back, Russ-son, you must show me

where TPM fits into TPS, number one. Number two, if I let you do this, you must be seen as the person representing TPS. You cannot lead a TPM steering committee."

After his return from Japan, Russ was ultimately able to show Fujio Cho how TPM not only fit into the Toyota production system but how consistent equipment availability was actually the foundation of the system. Yet, as promised, Cho would not allow Russ, because of his position in the organization, to lead TPM; he needed to continue to be seen as the leader of only TPS.

This story demonstrates protection because Cho essentially protected Russ from the negative consequences of being seen as the leader of TPM when he needed to be seen as the leader of TPS. This also demonstrates the importance of executive leadership in Russ's position to lead TPS. Cho emphasized TPS as a system and did not want to confuse the organization with multiple initiatives seemingly coming from Russ, the highest-level American leader in the powertrain division.

Story Number Seven: Participant Experienced Negative Japanese Emotion
This story shows how a sensei protected his protégé from an anticipated difficult emotionally charged situation.

The executive directors of production, control and some of the other departments where I presented something and that's the first time, I saw emotion come out of a Japanese. He slammed his fist down and made some comment. I had already been coached on that comment and the response by [my mentor, who] looked up at me, that's all he did, I gave my response that he coached me on 'cause he knew this was coming, then put his head back down . . . they [the Japanese] do get passionate, only when they're amongst themselves though. They would never show that to us because that was not what they wanted to teach us. Again, incredible discipline not to do that.

In this story, the American was coached on the anticipated comment before the meeting; the mentor had not only predicted the tough question from the Japanese but also coached the American on how to respond. This type of mentoring behavior, therefore, fits into the "protection" characteristic of a mentoring relationship.

Story Number Eight: Come With What You Have

In this story, Jeff Merriss was hired as a team member, promoted to team leader, and promoted again to junior engineer, and had an informal relationship with a Japanese leader—Art Niimi. In terms of protection, it appeared as though Art was protecting Jeff from negative emotional experiences by giving him mini-projects in anticipation of a big model change Jeff would be leading. The three lessons that Art was teaching Jeff at the time were:

1. Don't overthink the project or problem being solved.
2. Get input from others and don't do it yourself.
3. Don't be late.

In his interview, Jeff stated that every day or so at about the same time he would go to Art's office for 10 to 30 minutes for his daily mentoring lesson as a junior engineer. One story, in particular, stands out because it was at a time when Jeff was transitioning from small projects in anticipation of a big model change. Although he couldn't recall the specific project, he was able to recall his shortcomings: he was overthinking the project, he was trying to do it all himself, and he was in danger of being late but thinking he could just move the schedule back.

Knowing that Jeff loved Japanese history and the famous Okazaki castle near Toyoda city, Art told Jeff a story about how the first Shogun, Tokugawa, came to power. According to Art, Tokugawa consolidated his armies while waiting for one of his units to arrive for the battle. Tokugawa sent word to his son, who was leading the unit. "Come with what you have." His son arrived, focused on the battle, won, and the rest was history.

Art was essentially using this story to protect Jeff from the negative consequences of thinking he could move his deadline. Jeff describes his learning beyond the lesson at hand:

> During my 25-year career at Toyota, I was never late on a single project, period. I did not always have the success that I wanted but I never missed a deadline. I have also passed this lesson on to the people that worked for me. In turn, they have never missed a schedule.

Story Number Nine: Protection From Negative Consequences of Failure

Jeff continues with another story about how his mentor and the Toyota philosophy protected him from the negative consequences of failure. Jeff's first design as an engineer, totally on his own but signed-off by his mentor, was of a dolly, a cart that pulled the engines from powertrain to assembly. Jeff thought he was going to be a hero—that guy that designed a dolly to make moving engines much easier. Unfortunately, the dolly broke an axle before it could be on-loaded from the fabricator. So, Jeff, being an ambitious young engineer, shipped the dolly back to the fabricator. He called the owner and had him bring in a couple of crews to fix the new dolly while he actually re-designed the dolly to be about half the original size. Jeff worked day and night over the weekend to fix the dolly, just in time for the Monday morning trial. Jeff describes his sensei's reaction:

> Monday morning, we unload the dolly at 5 a.m., the trial started at 7, by this time I've been up like 48 hours and I was covered with black soot and grime. So [my sensei] comes in, and I walk up to his desk and he is sitting there, writing like he always does, and I said, "Kaz, I got the dolly in."
>
> He said, "How did it go?"
>
> I said, "It was a piece of shit."
>
> And he just kind of started grinning.
>
> I said, "You knew that when you signed it off."
>
> He said, "Yeah."
>
> At this point, Jeff thought he was going to get screamed at or even fired because his mistake cost

a few thousand dollars. The conversation continued:

He said, "You knew that it was a piece of crap, yet you let me do it anyway?"

Kaz said, "Will you ever do that again?"

"Hell no!"

Kaz smiled. "Cheap lesson."

Essentially, Jeff was permitted to fail, even if Toyota had to invest a few thousand dollars into a failure with hopes that he wouldn't repeat the same or similar mistakes. Jeff noted that his sensei had the patience to believe in him and let him fail, which began to soften the arrogance of this young engineer and improve his management style.

This story in particular stands in stark contrast to Jeff's previous story of Art protecting him from failure, while in this story Kaz essentially encouraged failure. Note the difference between Jeff's lesson on not being late, which would have negatively affected the entire large project and potentially cost Toyota a significant amount of time and money, and the failure of the dolly, which did not impact production or cause a large-scale problem.

Summary of Emotionally Charged Stories

All of these stories of protection showed an unanticipated theme of the research: the extent to which the Japanese senseis protected the Americans from negative emotional experiences, from fear of failure, and from the negative consequences of failure. The narratives of various emotionally charged experiences yielded the theme of protection—mainly the sensei protecting his protégé from actual or potential negative experiences and consequences. This is evidence that the coordinator-American relationship is properly categorized as a mentoring relationship. This is consistent with the literature, and both the oyabun-kobun and senpai-kohai mentoring relationships in Japan are characterized by "protection," the only key word found characterizing both types of relationships (Bright, 2005). Table 11 provides a summary of the stories that relate to the theme of "Protection." The table identifies the nature of the emotional experience for each, the underlying context, and the reasons these stories were chosen.

Table 11

Emotional Experiences

	Potentially Negative or Emotional Experience Involving Sensei	Underlying Context	Why is this Protection?
1	*Americans experience frustration* with Japanese lack of emotion.	The Japanese wanted to demonstrate rational behavior and keep emotional behaviors behind closed doors.	Seemingly a group effort on the part of the Japanese to protect Americans from negative emotions.

CHAPTER FOUR RESULTS 145

	Potentially Negative or Emotional Experience Involving Sensei	Underlying Context	Why is this Protection?
2	American leader protecting the workforce and the Japanese coordinator from the Japanese coordinator's emotions. *(Note, this is a weak story of protection, but was included because of the emotion involved.)*	Purposeful defects on cars accidentally shipped by Toyota, and the Japanese coordinator became very emotional.	American attempted to protect others from the negative experience and emotions of the Japanese coordinator.
3	Frustration of American worker when non-mentor Japanese trainer tried to train him on specific equipment.	Frustration essentially caused by the language barrier and additional stress.	His dedicated sensei quickly calmed him and removed him from the situation.
4	Mentee stopped production so he could inspect cars with a group leader prior to cars going to the next process step. Japanese non-dedicated executive coordinator of body shop yelled at mentee, asking why he stopped production.	Misunderstanding of stopping production to support quality.	Dedicated executive coordinator stepped in and corrected the other Japanese coordinator's negative behavior.
5	Protection from Inadvertent Neglect of Team Members	Participant's sensei points out socialization with the same team members on break, potentially neglecting other team members.	Japanese coordinator attempts to eliminate future consequences of favoring certain team members.

	Potentially Negative or Emotional Experience Involving Sensei	Underlying Context	Why is this Protection?
6	Introduction of Total Preventative Maintenance (TPM) at Toyota Powertrain.	Participant wanted to introduce TPM to Powertrain in Georgetown, KY. The Japanese mentor allowed this but did not permit him to lead the effort because he needed to be seen as the leader of TPS, not TPM.	The participant (General Manager) was protected from the negative consequences of being associated with both TPS and TPM.
7	Participant experienced negative Japanese emotion for the first time.	His Japanese mentor had already coached him on the question and the answer to the conversation causing negative emotion.	Sensei protected mentee by preparing and coaching him on the appropriate response to reduce further emotion from other Japanese leaders.
8	Come with what you have.	Participant was guided by Japanese mentor that timing was more important than perfection.	Japanese mentor was protecting the participant from the negative consequences of being late for a major line change at Toyota.
9	Protection from Negative Consequences of Failure.	Participant creates an improvement idea, which failed miserably and cost several thousand dollars.	Japanese coordinator created the environment where it was OK to fail and protected the participant after he failed.

The Mentoring Process

The second research question of the study was: "What are common steps for early American leaders transitioning from the initiation phase to the cultivation phase of the mentoring relationship?"

This section is primarily based on transcripts from John Allen, one of the first Americans hired to Toyota Georgetown. The transcript of John's interview was edited for clarity and intermixed with stories and quotes from others to elaborate certain points. From John's point of view, as an early American leader in the Human Resources group, John's interview essentially captured the initiation phase of the relationship between the Japanese coordinators and the early American mentees.

Keywords were used within the initiation and cultivation phases to extract stories and further categorize them. Nearly 300 keywords (watch, teach, grow, etc.) were extracted from the participants and placed into the following categories: *Americanizing TPS, Hiring Process, Learning to See, Perfect the Standard, Challenge, Questioning, Self-Learning, Becoming a* Sensei, *Promotion, Mutual Trust/Respect,* and *Other.* Figure 10 portrays what seems to be the process and phases of the sensei-protégé relationship at Toyota based on Kram (1983) and participant interviews. Additionally, these steps seem to align first with Scientific Management (learn and perfect the one best way) and then quality improvement theory (improve the one best way by iterative cycles of improvement, i.e. PDCA). Protégés seem to move from initiation to cultivation when they are able to apply the knowledge of quality management beyond the specific problem at hand to a point of self-learning on how to ask themselves the questions a sensei would ask.

Figure 10

The Process From Initiation to Cultivation at Toyota

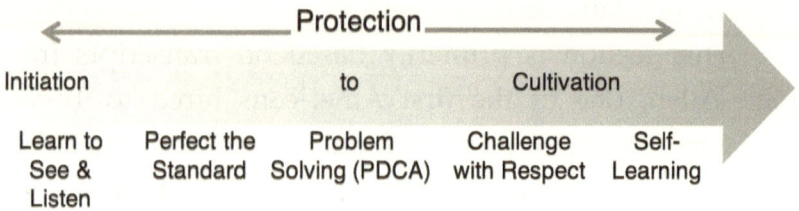

Initiation and Scientific Management

The word "initiation" in reference to the first phase of mentor relationships is described by Kram (1983), but is also an accurate word to describe the beginning of the journey by the "Group of 26," the 26 Americans who were the first group leaders at Toyota Georgetown. Generally, they were taught by the Japanese on how to see to the actual process by standing in the circle—a process of standing in a chalk-drawn circle to observe the process deeply. Then, in order to learn their specific jobs, they were taught to perfect the standard, so the jobs were performed the one best way known.

Though they saw quality improvement in action during their time in Japan, the emphasis seemed to be first on standardized work. Then, once the work was understood, they could apply problem solving to fix problems and improve the standardized work. This systemization included the "Three Rights" (right place, time, and tools), written work instructions for each task including timing for each work element, and economic incentives. The elimination of waste mindset of scientific management seemed to be built into Toyota when the Group of 26 arrived in Japan (Tompkins, 2005).

The first group of Americans was sent to Japan in July before the plant in Georgetown was scheduled for completion. The Japanese hoped the visit would be an orientation to the company and tried to give the Americans as much information as possible, but even they did not really understand what was in store for the newly hired Americans. At that point, when the Japanese took the new group leaders to Japan, the Japanese basically said to their U.S. HR people, "Thank you very much for your efforts. But we have our process for doing this," signaling that the Japanese had a pre-determined plan of initiation for the newly hired Americans.

Learning to See and Listen

On the very first day of their visit to Japan, leaders within Toyota introduced the group of 26 Americans to the Toyota Production System. One of those was David Meier, co-author of *The Toyota Way Fieldbook* (Liker & Meier, 2005) and *Toyota Talent* (Liker & Meier, 2007). The day was extremely hot, the newly hired Americans were tired and jet-lagged but were about to learn their new roles within Toyota. One of the first lessons was about the elements of TPS. David was especially interested in what was about to happen because his Master's thesis focused on the use of automation, he had studied Japanese manufacturing superiority, and had previously studied Toyota from an academic standpoint.

David and others within the group of 26 Americans

began to learn TPS in a three-day training session that was intended to ingrain TPS into the new hires. As David described it:

> In comes this guy. "My name is Mr. So and So, I'm the General Manager of Production Control, and I'm gonna tell you about TPS . . . Toyota Production System . . . standardized work . . . blah blah blah blah."
>
> The second guy comes in. "My name is Mr. So and So, I'm the General Manager of the Quality Department," and he starts talking about standardized work, and blah blah blah—same stuff. I'm like okay that's kind of what the last guy said.
>
> Then comes another guy. "My name is Mr. So and So, I'm the General Manager of such and such department," and he starts talking about standardized work and blah blah blah. After about the third or fourth guy [I'm thinking], "What the hell, they're all saying the same thing." I look around the room and the guys are sitting there like this [holding his eyes open with his fingers], I mean literally trying to hold their eyes open, it's hot, we're jet-lagged, these guys keep saying the same thing. So, this, I think it went on for a couple of days.

The point of this story is that Toyota's approach to initiation—to both Toyota and the sensei—was above all about the Toyota Production System, a lesson that was repeated again and again by different Toyota managers during the initial orientation.

CHAPTER FOUR RESULTS 151

Standing in the Circle

One early American leader said, "Starting from day one, everybody gets the 'Ohno Circle,' when they join the company." This is how Toyota teaches its people to look more deeply through observation of the manufacturing floor by standing in a chalk-drawn circle or on a chalk-drawn X on the floor, a method attributed to Taiichi Ohno. Five of seven interviewees spontaneously told stories about this experience, and four of them described this as a significant "aha" moment. Note, standing in a circle was not unique to this group and was noted by participants in other situations as well. As one of the early American managers said:

> Probably the most important "aha!" moment for me was learning to see that moment in my career where my sensei . . . would just take you to a point and say, "Stand there and tell me what you see." [After several iterations of "keep looking"] they would try to make you see behaviors versus results. That was probably one of the greatest "aha!" moments I would say, it's learning to see."

But learning to see was not easy and came with its frustrations. The following story demonstrates the frustration of standing in a circle until the purpose was understood and more meaningful interactions could occur. David Meier tells his story:

> "Here's Mr. Honda, he's gonna be your trainer while you're in Japan." [On the first day in the factory] he draws an X on the floor with a piece of chalk and he says, "You looking, okay?"

"Yeah, what am I looking for? What's the point of this exercise?"

And he's like, "Yeah, it's looking."

I said, "No, what am I looking for?"

And he says, "What?"

I said, "Yes, what. What am I looking for?"

He says, "Yes, looking."

I said, "No, what am I looking for?"

He says, "What?"

I say, "Yes, what? What am I looking for?"

Ten minutes into this I'm thinking this is not working, guy can't even tell me what the hell I'm supposed to—he draws an X on the floor and says look at this, and what. So, finally, probably about ten minutes or so, I just thought screw it, whatever, looking, I mean how hard can looking be, so I'm standing there, and he disappears, and he doesn't come back for two hours.

Mr. Honda smoked like a chimney, so I figured he's on a smoke break or something, he finally comes back after two hours and I learned since he didn't speak a lot of English I can sort of give him a hard time and he's not gonna know what I'm saying.

I'm like, "Where the hell did you go? You leave me standing here, I don't know where the bathroom is. I don't know where anything is."

And he says, "Dave-San, what see?"

"Well, this guy is doing this and this, and blah blah." I give him a run down.

He says, "Oh okay, more looking."

Go back to the same question. "Okay, what is it I'm supposed to be looking for? Cause I've been standing here for two hours, you left me here, I don't know what the point of this is, what, help me out here, what am I supposed to...?"

And it was the same. "Yes, looking."

I'm like, "Looking, what?"

"What?"

"Yes, what am I looking for?"

Went through that whole conversation again, same thing, not getting anywhere so by then, I'm just, seriously, spent 3 days in the classroom listening to person after person after person spend 4 hours saying the same thing that the last guy said for 3 frickin' days. Now I'm out in the plant, I think I've got a month to learn everything, we're 4 days in and I haven't learned shit, okay. And he's got me standing here looking for what God knows, I have no clue and I'm trying to figure out what the [explicative] is this all about, this is just nuts, and when are we gonna get down to learning something?

So literally the second two hours I'm standing there 'cause I've already looked and I've already saw, I don't know, I'm literally thinking to myself, where is the bathroom? Did I make a mistake? Wonder if I can get my old job back? I wonder if I can even find my way out of this country 'cause I have no idea where I am 'cause they just drive me over here, all these thoughts going through my head, I mean, I'm ready to go back taking my old job 'cause I don't know what the hell, this is just crazy, here I'm standing.

He comes back again two hours later and says same thing.

"Dave-San, what see?"

"I already told you." (In Kentucky, I would say, "Already done told ya.") And I explained it again.

He said, "More looking."

I'm like, "What the hell am I supposed to see?"

And I'm, you know by this time I'm just like you have got to be freakin' kidding me but something comes to mind, I think, okay . . . I can record this, and you know, I've done time studies, I can do some analysis on this work, and how, started out from day one. I'll impress him, and he'll let me off this damn X because I don't know what's it gonna take to get off this damn X but apparently, I'm not getting it.

So, I'm making notes, two hours came, same thing, he comes back, asked me, "What see?"

I say, "Okay, let me show you," I'm laying it all out. I'm showing him.

"Mm, very good, very good."

I'm thinking, "Finally!"

He says, "More looking."

What the hell, right? What's it gonna take? So the day goes by, completely exhausted because standing in one place for 8 hours is a lot of work, it's very difficult, trying to figure out what the hell the lesson's supposed to be, trying to figure out how the heck do I get off from that stupid X and get down to work that I'm thinking I'm supposed to be doing, I'm wasting my time and I haven't learned a damn thing yet, right?

So, I get back to all the other guys, and they're all like, "What did you do today?"

"I stood there all day looking, what's that, what are we, why are we doing that?"

"I don't know."

Some guys had to stand for two days 'cause they didn't get it.

The lesson for David came to him years later: the point was to learn how to observe things and to understand deeply. As he learned from later experiences, people tend to come to a superficial understanding of something, to declare that they understand it, and move on to the next thing. This is exactly what he and the other Americans did many times, observing while standing in the circle and at other times simply observing.

The point of observing, though, according to David, is not necessarily the specifics of what a person sees. It is to deeply understand the situation, which is a skill in and of itself. Deeply understanding the situation takes time, especially for those in the initiation phase of the relationship. As David elaborated, "You don't learn by somebody telling you what you gonna learn, you learn by going through that experience yourself."

During the trip to Japan, the Americans observed the actual process, along with problem solving, and celebrations. Catesby Prewitt describes an example of problem solving:

> I can remember was they had a, at the plant in Japan, they had a power failure. It was a high voltage cable that they had, and it was running in a trial for wires and cabling was there and it shorted, and short blew up and shut the plant down. So, I remember that exercise that they were involved in that problem. What caused the failure and they went to a problem solving exercise: why? why? why? ... And was able

to determine root cause for that failure and then implement the appropriate countermeasures. I can't really remember those specifics but I'm just sitting here now, trying to visualize that cable they showed pictures of and then what they did to prevent it from happening again.

David describes an example of a best practice that began with his Japanese coordinator asking, "Would you guys like to see a die change?"

I'm sitting there like, holy crap, this is gonna be a while. You know, the thing is ten times bigger than our machine, I can only imagine how many hours it's gonna take. It took my guy [back home] 4 hours to change the dye that was this big, these ones are as big as a car, right.

And he says, "Okay, is everybody ready?"

I'm like, "Yeah, okay,"

He blows a whistle. I'm like what the heck is he blowing a whistle for? Next thing I know it's finished. Like, what the hell just happened? I'm like, do that again. "What?" Come on, I thought we were gonna be here for like 2 weeks. And in 5 minutes, it's done.

And finally John describes a celebration.

He didn't tell me about any of the work they'd done. At the end of it, [it was all done in Japanese], they celebrated wildly! I mean it was a real celebration! I turned to the person that was with me then . . . and basically said to him, "Wow, they must have really saved a lot of time on that operation!"

He said, "Yeah, we save a quarter of a second!"

These stories demonstrate that the Japanese were following an established plan for classroom training, standing in the circle, and observing for the Americans during their first trip to Japan.

Perfect the Standard

The way participants described perfecting the standard resonated with Scientific Management theory: dividing tasks, determining the one best way, training workers in that one best way (Tompkins, 2005). John continues to describe the Initiation process from learning to see to perfecting the standard. After learning to see, the Americans engaged in a 30-day process referred to as *My Own Process* (MOP) training. One humbling yet practical purpose of MOP was for the new hires to experience what their team members would experience: hard work, getting tired and sore. One participant noted his high stress levels at this time because he thought the purpose was to completely learn the job in 30 days and that there would be no help back in America.

The primary purposes of the MOP training according to John were twofold: to demonstrate that when they returned to America there was to be a very strict, regimented, almost military way that they and others would have to work and to demonstrate that the Americans must first learn and perfect the established standard before making any suggestion on how to improve the work.

At Toyota Georgetown, John Allen noted that it took three years before the plant had a suggestion system. That's how long the Japanese thought it would take the Americans to understand that a standard is a standard, and the standard will be followed no matter what. And when someone can't follow the standard for whatever reason, there will be people there to help that person through the system.

In spite of the traditional nature of Japanese culture, enough of the modern had infused itself into Japanese life that Toyota leaders were afraid that the Americans would lose what was really unique and different about Toyota. So, just like boot camp, as John called it, Toyota Georgetown at first would take everything away from you and then build you into a "soldier." The Americans were to learn that if they weren't marching together, disorganization and chaos would soon follow. In these boot camps at Georgetown, anyone brought in at any entry level was thrown into this status free society that Toyota was creating. Not everyone would make it through boot camp, of course. But once you made it through, you could go back to whatever specialty or status got you hired by Toyota in the first place—in a sense free to start your career. Recruits at Toyota were heavily and deeply indoctrinated.

John recounts that an American's first job was usually not in his or her area of expertise. Although this was real work, it was not really the beginning of a career at Toyota. As David elaborates:

Archie called me up one night, he says, "Well, we gonna offer you a job at Toyota, in plastics."

I said, "Archie, I don't know anything about plastics." I was confused, I thought they'd put me on body weld or stamping, 'cause that's my background was metals, factory, plant that I worked at, we did metal fab.

He said, "That's okay, they'll teach you what you need to know."

Initiation Summary

Generally, the process of initiation seemed to involve three steps: learn to see through standing in a circle, perfect the standard, and solve problems with the Japanese coordinator. All three steps seemed to be a part of the initiation phase and aligned with Scientific Management, learning the one best way, and then applying problem solving to improve the one best way. Once the mentee learned to see and think deeply, beyond the specific task and problem at hand, they had the opportunity to apply the lessons from Japanese problem solving to other scenarios, the relationship with the sensei then began to shift from initiation to cultivation.

Cultivation

As discussed in Chapter 2, the turning point into the cultivation phase takes place when both individuals benefit from the relationship, when opportunities for meaningful interaction occur, and when an emotional bond deepens. Characteristics include frequent and meaningful interactions, strong relationships both professionally and personally, transformative learning, a highly productive relationship, and mutual growth. The most obvious themes marking the turning points into cultivation and cultivation itself are when the protégé learns how to extend problem solving concepts beyond the immediate problem, eventually becoming a self-learner. This section focuses on how coordinators used problem solving and challenging assignments to teach protégés lessons as successful relationships turned into self-learning.

Problem Solving

The concept of root cause problem solving was taught immediately after the standards were understood. For a new employee at Toyota, the experience is almost like boot camp—much like the original group of managers experienced in Japan. The employee first goes through orientation, then training for about a year—the whole year is spent on learning problem solving within the Toyota Production System. The challenge of problem solving seems to be the bridge between the initiation and cultivation phases of mentoring.

The first step of problem solving is identifying the problem; as one American manager describes it:

> Every time you were faced with something, they [the Japanese coordinators] would challenge you to be able to identify the Five Why's, asking "Why?" five times to find the root cause of a problem. And they would not move production until that Five Why's was clear, until you knew you were at the point of cause.

This type of in-process problem solving seemed to have been influenced by Deming and Juran's Quality Management Theory. Statistical process control relies on preventing quality errors, as opposed to inspection and correction, and Toyota taught its newly hired Americans to do problem solving in the form of the five-whys as problems occurred — asking "why" in sequence until one finds the root cause of the problem. The purpose of problem solving, though, seemed to be both operational and developmental: solve the problem at hand so it doesn't happen again and improve the quality of a mentee's thinking. After problems were identified, the Americans needed to come up with countermeasures or long-term solutions to ensure the problem did not happen again. The first several times they tried to solve the problem, the Japanese coordinators would say, "Not good," and throw it back to them. This was to deliver the message: "You're not thinking deeply enough." This message is the counterpart of the message taught when standing in a circle: "You're not observing deeply enough."

The Americans would keep trying, believing that questioning was an iterative thing, only to find out that it's about the *quality of thinking*. Once it was clear to the Japanese coordinators, through constant questioning and challenging, that the American leader was seeing and thinking deeply enough, the Americans were, in a sense, now ready for their careers at Toyota. These Americans essentially moved from the initiation phase to the cultivation phase of the mentoring relationship based on the deep development of their thinking. The following describes what that process was actually like for some Americans:

> The lessons, the daily lessons, [such as] correcting a memo 13 times before they would actually approve it . . . and . . . I never did anything without 4 or 5 questions. . . . That just showed me the discipline and the detail that they were willing to maintain that level

without me wearing them down; they were gonna wear *me* down.

The problem-solving process used by the senseis that built mutual trust and respect while simultaneously teaching the process to their protégés followed a specific order.

1. Assess the current situation relative to the expectation.
2. Go and see with humility.
3. Reiterate that mistakes are OK and how can I help you?
4. Come to consensus on an improvement.
5. Grasp the situation well enough to delegate it.
6. Make a plan and monitor the situation.

In John's words:

You know, I start thinking about leadership, and I start looking back at what's actually happened, I realize that there were some patterns that were there. First thing you have to do is assess the current situation and where are you relative to what's expected, either short-term or long-term. The next thing you have to do is go and see. Part of going and seeing, and the really important part of that, is to show up at that place as humble. If you don't show up as humble, you're going to push something, there will be resistance. If you show up and basically say, "How can I help you?" or "I'm sorry you had a mistake," then you get a different kind of relationship. You have this humility, which is the fundamental part of being a citizen in Toyota is that you're basically humble.

You're not bragging about what you're doing right, right? You're constantly trying to improve and do better.

As you go through, you have to make sure that you understand the situation well enough to delegate it. Once you delegate it, you have to be able to monitor the planning that's going on and make sure that that happens. It's all a PDCA [Plan-Do-Check-Act] cycle.

John is referring to Shewhart's PDCA Cycle and generally Quality Improvement Theory, and the process described mirrored that of Deming and Juran's PDCA: develop a quality improvement project (plan), introduce a small-scale change to test the improvement (do); determine whether the anticipated improvement actually happened and to what extent (check); and introduce broader more permanent changes based on the improvement results (act) (Tompkins, 2005).

John continues to expand on PDCA and on how leaders manage and delegate the PDCA cycle:

> Except for a manager and a leader, it's CAPCDA [Check-Act-Plan-Do-Check-Act]. And so, but they have to do this in a certain way that leaves people with the good feeling that the manager is there to help them, and the good feeling that not trying to catch them doing something wrong. Quite the contrary. If you make mistakes, this is great. We'll figure out how to keep that from ever happening again. So, all this stuff, this background fits together, and the whole process of making the car. And the result of

that is that every car is to standard, and if it's not to standard, then it's rigorous problem solving, trying to figure out why.

That's the kind of system thinking that goes on. . . . But the few pieces, the small pieces there, the proper assessment of the current situation, showing up as a person who is humble and wants to help make things happen, are very important to establishing this thing called mutual trust and respect.

Challenging

The concept of further challenging beyond problem solving seemed to be the next step within the cultivation phase of the mentoring relationship. Based on an analysis of the interviews, participants were challenged both in the initiation phase and the cultivation phase. The distinguishing factor seemed to be if the mentee could apply the lesson beyond the immediate situation. This signified a change in the relationship as well as a change in the protégé's thinking.

The purpose of annual planning at Toyota was to create an improvement plan to achieve improved targeted measures. David, a group leader, and Russ, a general manager, describe the challenging process of the annual plan and how it improved the thinking of the Americans.

> The planning process to get there [hitting the targeted number] I think is difficult, and I really hated [it . . . and] . . . I'd procrastinate to the very end and then sit down and make something up because I knew that the plan wasn't gonna come true and that's why

I hated doing it.

It's like how the heck am I supposed to figure out all the details of something and, it's not gonna work out that way. And so, I was telling you the story, the sensei is telling me you know, I'm going: "Why are we doing this?"

And he's saying, "Very important."

And I'm saying, "But the plan is wrong?"

He said, "Yup, always wrong, plan is always wrong."

I'm like, "Well, if it's always wrong then why are we doing this?"

"Planning is very important."

"But it's wrong."

"Yes, always wrong."

"But then why are we doing this. . . ." This was the kind of conversation I had all the time. "Well, I'm confused on this lesson. Here you're telling me this is very important but you're telling me it's always wrong, how do you remedy those two things?"

David describes that it was only later that the different pieces fell into place as he recalled one of Toyota's mantras: "The plan is worthless, but the planning is priceless." He summed up the lesson by adding, "On one hand, the plan is not as good as the paper it's written on, but the process of planning is extremely important."

Russ describes how the concept of challenging is built into the Toyota Production System so that top-level leadership can directly challenge the entire workforce to achieve certain targets using a "Thrust Month" through the suggestion system:

> One thing Toyota is extremely good at is rewards and recognition, not necessarily money per se but they always had things going on to reward and recognize team members, it's just a constant thing. Mr. Cho had a luncheon, once a quarter we as general managers, Mike Dodge and myself had to nominate teams not that won the biggest suggestion award, had put the most ingenuity into their suggestions, may have been very small monetary awards but it took a lot of thinking.
>
> And Mr. Cho would hold this luncheon with those teams, thank them, give them a plaque and it had their names on and stuff, they admired that. I always loved, everyone had to wear a baseball cap, I had to wear a baseball cap. Team members when they had a suggestion that was accepted and implemented, of which they had to be part of the implementation and leaders verify the work was complete. They were awarded a little half an inch, Kentucky State pin, really the team members as far as I was convinced at the time, did not care at all about the monetary award of the suggestion, it was a competition to see who would get more pins in their hats. It reminded me of the Ohio State Buckeyes and their helmets. You

had team members with 60/70/80 pins on their hat, and they start fresh every year, so I thought that was alright.

Then they would have a thing called the Thrust month, where they would either have a safety target, or they'd have a sales target or a quality target, and they would challenge everybody to get involved. Those were Thrust months; they had those several times a year.

Self-Learning

One characteristic of the cultivation phase of the mentor relationship is transformative learning. Merriam-Webster defines "transform" as: "to change in composition or structure; to change the outward form or appearance of; and to change in character or condition" (Transform, n.d.). The following stories from participants demonstrate a transformation into self-learning.

Russ, as the General Manager and highest-level American leader at Toyota, noted that the Japanese, in particular, President Cho, taught him how to question:

> [During the first six weeks in Japan] when they [the Japanese] trained us on things like standardized work and problem solving, they did not train, at least at my level, they did not train it so much to be an implementer. They trained it more from being a questioner. So, they did not necessarily care that I couldn't go out and train standardized work. The training of these tools were all by the team leaders

and group leaders after a Train the Trainer class for them. I had to understand standardized work and other TPS tools for what they were and how to go question it.

And so, I did very little problem solving per se. But I went through a lot of problem solving reviews. And, you knew the steps that we had, and you knew how to challenge them. And then they [those solving the problem] could take you over to the data, where they got it [the information to solve the problem].

David explains that many people believe that the concept of "learn by doing" has the emphasis on the word "doing" versus the word "learn." It took him years to realize that the operative word was learn and that self-learning is the goal of a mentor-mentee relationship:

> So again, it was learn by doing and I thought *doing* was the operative word and that the result that we achieved was the intention, and it took me forever to realize that *learn* was the operative word, that they were giving us challenges so that we learn how to improve processes, and how to think, and how to have a thinking process.
>
> The strange thing looking back on it, yet they were telling us over and over again, it's all about the process, we don't want luck, they would say, we want to have a process, that's more likely, they wouldn't say guaranteed, but more likely to give us an outcome that we desire, right. And so, Americans we

say, "a blind squirrel can find a nut now and then," and that's what they said they were trying to avoid. They did not want accidentally or lucky or somehow to achieve some outcome, they wanted to, you had a process that you went through, also known as the problem solving process, right, the thinking process.

Russ Scaffede further describes that his responsibility as taught to him by Fujio Cho was not to solve the problem but to quiz the questions and always compare to the standard. Russ describes this experience as a turning point in his thinking:

> Typically, in the West, we'd throw out some ideas or we would think of the answer, especially if you're an executive. [Mr. Cho] . . . was far more humble and you're with him, and he's quizzing the team to how did they come up with their solution, show me the status of the chart that you're tracking to make sure it happened or what's your next thought of thinking if it's not working. . . .
>
> What Mr. Cho taught me very clearly . . . was questioning: have you questioned the group leaders that they see where this waste is, are they working on that waste, how are they going about trying to eliminate it? He did not come up with any solutions, he always quizzed and enquired, which was a very significant teaching and very hard to do. Even when team members made an improvement, they were taught to be capable to show the original standard they were com-

paring against. During my years at GM I might have been taught to get the first-line supervisor and say: "Thanks for the improvement, however, very rare was this compared to any standard and often did not make a total improvement for the plant, just my area!"

One time early on Mr. Cho said: "Russ-San, I want to come to the plant floor, and I want to see any improvement you and your team members want me to see. But before you do that, there is one thing you must do for me—you must teach them to show me the standard they're comparing against, because if they can't show me the standard, they can't verify whether they've made an improvement or didn't."

And actually, he went into one of these dissertations and sometimes you think: "Oh man, what's going on?" Cause he said one of three things happened, and this was just walking the floor one day, he said, "They either made an improvement, cleaned the area up, moved a lot of things around, possibly painted some stuff up, they're very proud of it but they can't show you how they've sustained and made the improvement. Or they've cleaned the place up, they've moved stuff around, they're very proud of what they've worked on the last weeks and months, but on what the original goal was—they've made no improvement at all." Then he went to the last one . . . "or have they really worked together, cleaned stuff up . . . and actually lost ground over the time on what they're trying to improve."

And I actually walked away scratching my head, honestly did think: "That's one of the goofiest conversations I've ever had." Then, honestly, I thought back to my years at General Motors. . . . I actually took my 18 plus years and went back and tabulated, and we should have been labor free by the time I left. We made that many productivity improvements year after year, but we just shuffled people round the plant, and his point was an improvement is: you can physically track it back and you've made an improvement for the plant. So, when I thought back, we did years and years and years of fooling ourselves and the teams that they made improvements.

This story was a turning point for Russ: one of the lessons learned is that when questioning, the mentor must question to ensure that the team has compared itself to a standard to verify if they've made an improvement or not.

David Meier tells a similar story of his coordinator questioning him using the same questions even though he improved beyond his expectations. This event occurred about four or five years into his journey at Toyota where I believe he started to understand the philosophy of no fault, no blame:

> So . . . this is probably 2 years into my experience, and I think, okay, they asked me to do this particular thing, if we achieve 20% more than that target, surely that's got to be the attaboy level, they got to acknowledge good job at that point, right?
>
> So, we set out and we worked really hard, and we

achieved 120% of the target, right? and my Japanese trainers just like "ano" [translated as "but"] and he starts asking questions.

I said: "Hold on, time out, maybe I didn't explain this well. Target achieved, over target."

And he's like, "Yes, but what did you miss?"

I'm like, "Maybe you missed the point," I said. So, the Japanese guys love baseball, so I tried to give them a baseball analogy, I'm like, you know, "home run—yaay." [David motions like he's hitting a home run in baseball.]

And he's like, "Yes, yes, yes, but what did you miss?"

"Maybe you're not getting the point." I said, "Try this one—base is loaded, grand slam, home run, yaay!"

He's like, "Yes but what did you miss?"

I'm like, "What the heck, what are you talking about? We didn't miss anything, we got 20% more than the goal, don't you understand, where is the congratulations, where is the good job thing," right?

And so as often was the case in my experience at Toyota when we reached that level, it was time to go get the translator, the interpreter because we weren't understanding each other.

So we go get the translator and he says something

to her in Japanese and basically she comes back and she says: "What he's saying is," and draw this on the board, "here's the goal, and what he's saying is, whether you hit the goal or fall short of the goal or you see the goal, makes no difference if you don't know how you got to where you got. The point is not where you got, the point is how did you get there, what was your thinking process?"

As I learned later, the reason they were asking all these questions wasn't because I did something wrong, it was because the only way I could understand your thought process is to ask you questions about your thought process, right? I can see the result of your efforts, but I can't understand the process you used to get to that effort, okay?

So that was the light bulb moment, it was like "holy crap!" that light bulb didn't go off until 10 years later, okay? But his point was, if you exceed the goal or fall short of the goal, what his point was, what did you miss in your thinking that you didn't see that potential? You achieved it but you didn't recognize it beforehand, right and part of the planning process is to anticipate what your outcome is gonna be and if you fall short or exceed that, obviously something was missing in your preliminary thinking process. . . .

[That] was sort of their way of conditioning you to understand continuous improvement, that regardless of what you just achieved and went through, great, what went on here and what was the process of what you used to get there wasn't so much where you got but it was how you got there. . . .

Regardless of what level you achieve because there is always something else, you know continuous improvement, I mean that's what it took me, the first rule says—continuous improvement implies that everything can be improved forever, there is no, unless you reach a state of perfection, which you never can, you can always get better. Maybe it's incrementally less but there is still some next level, right?

Jeff Merriss explains his final turning point that removed the chip from his shoulder, which took several years:

When I finally turned a corner to where I became a good, I don't know, employee or understood the Japanese style, and really brought out my management style is where we, after every project we did a reflection. Small project, big project, it didn't matter. We had the discipline in those first six years to do that.

And what I learned is, American style is—you do a reflection, you know everyone does a reflection, you know, do a model launch for GM and they tell you we did this, we were perfect, we were great, and they don't tell you [the problems]. Japanese is totally different. They are: we don't care what you did well, we wanna know what could you improve on. So, after a lot of little projects where they would remind you to bring this out, and you had to re-write it and say okay this could have been better, they didn't judge you by that, they celebrated that and said: "Yeah, that's good."

So once we did a big project and we did plant 2, and plant 2 was a major project, it was another, we had a 100,000,000 dollar budget, we had six engineers, and I was on that project and we had a four-page reflection and by that time I was confident enough that then we could say: "We missed this, we missed this, we missed this," and there wasn't gonna be finger-pointing, at least not by the Japanese. . . .

That really was the point where I could say, the chip is off my shoulder because you can point a finger at me, I don't care, we can have this, then I truly understood what the Japanese were trying to explain to us, when in the early years we were pointing fingers and you know, you did this, and you didn't do this, and they would just calmly sit there and reassure us. Then I could sit in the meeting and say, "I did this," and they could come at me and point fingers, and I'd say, "Yeah, absolutely." So yeah, so that was my personal learning point.

These stories demonstrate that mentoring at Toyota occurred within a no-fault no-blame environment. The senseis would challenge the Americans no matter the result. They would challenge the Americans if they did not achieve the target, if they did achieve the target, or if they exceeded the target. The specific questions may have been different, like, for example: "What did you miss in the planning process to not achieve the target? or "What did you miss in the planning process that you underestimated what you could achieve?" Both stories are a clear demonstration that mentoring the Toyota Way is rooted in challenging and not rooted simply achieving or not achieving targets.

Turning Points to Cultivation

The above stories not only point out how to challenge and think within TPS with the mentor being the primary instigator, but they also reflect significant turning points in the mentee's relationship with the mentor and the Toyota organization. As shown in Figure 10, senseis challenged protégés to improve standardized work through iterative cycles of PDCA and other challenges. As David describes, the emphasis in the phrase "learn by doing" is on the word "learn." The point of challenging within the Toyota Production System, whether problem solving, generating improvements, or creating an annual plan, is to become a self-learner outside of the sensei-protégé relationship, always applying quality management with respect. Once quality management thinking is solidified, it can be applied outside of the specific task at hand and eventually without the guidance of a mentor. This transition from being able to apply quality management thinking beyond the improvement at hand, seems to be a critical turning point into cultivation and then self-learning.

Additionally, when making an improvement, whether the protégé falls short of or exceeds the target, the same questions must be asked because the outcome was not the expected outcome. This, again, implies that quality management thinking transcends the task at hand and includes the overall thought process put into the actual improvement efforts. The mentor must ask the protégé questions so the mentee better reflects on future challenges and has the potential to instill quality management thinking.

As Russ learned from Mr. Cho, improvements must always be compared to the standard to determine if there was actually an improvement. Regardless, as Jeff notes, bad news comes first, last, and always, because discussions must be around challenges—what did not work and why, so further improvement can be made, thus improving the thinking of the protégé. As Russ noted, an environment of mutual trust and respect is necessary for this transparent form of questioning.

In such a challenging and vulnerable environment, not everyone was able to move from the initiation phase to the cultivation phase. Some compared the first few years at Toyota to military training. Survival meant you came out a better person, but not everyone made it. After constant challenges and questioning, David Meier recognized that many people were stuck in the loop of challenging and questioning by the Japanese coordinators, but weren't learning:

> I recognize a lot of people who are stuck in that loop [not learning by doing], waiting for the sensei or somebody to come tell them what to do. And they never get out of that loop because they don't understand: the point is not the doing, the point is the learning. And if you're not learning that lesson to be able to apply it in another scenario, you're not learning anything."

Participants noted that some early American leaders were able to act the part, but never truly change, even if they were able to act as if they changed. These people would behave a certain way when the Japanese were around, then reverted to bad behaviors of table pounding, yelling, and swearing.

Cultivating Quality Management

As discussed in Chapter 2, quality management theory is built upon scientific management. Likewise, Toyota senseis seemed to use the scientific management technique of learning and teaching the one best way to perform a process before instilling a quality management mindset, as described in the Initiation Phase of Figure 10. The PDCA cycle was used in both the initiation phase to teach how to improve those specific work processes, and continually improve the "one best way." PDCA, discussed in Chapter 2, includes: develop a quality improvement project (Plan); introduce a small-scale change to test the improvement (Do); determine whether the anticipated improvement actually happened and to what extent (Check); and introduce broader more permanent changes based on the improvement results (Act).

PDCA and quality management thinking was used by senseis in both the initiation and cultivation phases to help reinforce this PDCA process until quality improvement thinking or a PDCA mindset was truly understood and applied by protégés, the actual turning point in the relationship. As shown in Figure 10, first the PDCA cycle was used for specific work processes, and more challenging of the protégé took place as the protégé matured in the relationship. As Total Quality Management was becoming a fad in American companies in the 1980s and 1990s, Toyota was actually using its best senseis to develop protégés within the Toyota Production System to instill a quality management mindset to the point of self-learning. This presumably helped Toyota become the world's top automaker, and the Toyota Production System become the envy many of organizations across a multitude of sectors.

Summary

Mandatory developmental relationships within Toyota, as previously defined, had several common characteristics. Overall, experiences were positive with the assigned Japanese mentors, especially in the initial three-year cycle prior to 1990. The age of the Japanese senseis was generally about the same or older than their U.S. protégés. Most participants acknowledged that their mentors had more knowledge about TPS and in some cases more technical knowledge but less knowledge about how to work with a U.S. workforce. The purpose of interactions was more general, and the duration depended on the level in the organization—three years for managers and rotating three months for group leaders. All participants noted that the medium of interaction was face-to-face. All participants noted that regularity of interactions was either scheduled or unscheduled within a mostly dyadic context, although some interactions were also in groups. These face-to-face relationships within the company were formal and structured, since they were established and defined by Toyota, but the interactions were generally informal and unstructured. All but one participant strongly agreed that both their senseis and Toyota were trustworthy. All participants noted that their relationship with their Japanese-mentor ended as planned after the rotation was up. Participants noted that all Japanese coordinators were male—as were the Americans—and weren't aware of any opposite gender relationships.

The stories of protection demonstrated that the Japanese senseis protected the Americans from negative emotional experiences, from fear of failure, and from the negative consequences of failure—both independently and also what seemed to be by design. This is evidence that the coordinator-American relationship is properly categorized as a mentoring relationship, consistent with the literature, and both the *oyabun-kobun* and *senpai-kohai* mentoring relationships in Japan are characterized by protection. Protection seems to be especially important when moving a mentor relationship from initiation to cultivation in any organization.

The mentoring process at Toyota Georgetown from initiation to cultivation may be replicated in other organizations. But focusing only on lean tools without applying the concepts of protection and challenging with respect may be contributing factors to the failures many organizations have faced in attempting to implement TPS. Initiation, from this study, includes learning to see and perfecting the standard. First, an organization or a work unit must standardize the one best way to accomplish the work. Standardized work is necessary for the protégé to test quality management, use PDCA, and actually make a plan to improve the process. Without standardized work, it will be difficult for sensei and protégé to collaborate, first to learn the work and then to improve that work systematically.

Cultivation seems to take hold after consistent application of PDCA via questioning and challenging by a sensei. Based on several stories, the act of challenging is a key concept to move the protégé from the initiation phase to the cultivation phase. This challenging, as in the cases of Russ, David, and others, was not simply about achieving targets but was about learning how to apply quality management and the PDCA cycle beyond the scope of the problem at hand. Russ's experience with Cho showed that Russ was not only learning the Toyota Production System but was also simultaneously learning how to challenge his own U.S. protégés so that they could learn from Russ as an American sensei. This demonstrates that even executive-level leaders new to quality management thinking can still be successful mentors by knowing how to challenge and how to ask questions in a context of mutual trust and respect that protects protégés from difficult emotional situations and unnecessary failure.

The initiation phase at Toyota Georgetown included learning to see and learning to listen, followed by perfecting the standard. The initiation phase integrates scientific management theory, specifically "determining the 'one best way' to perform each task, train workers in the 'one best way,' [and] measure their performance . . ." (Tompkins, 2005, p. 67). In terms of the cultivation phase, the data suggests that the purpose of challenging is to bring the protégé to a point of self-learning and the application of a quality management mindset. Part of this process was inculcating aspects of quality management theory, specifically PDCA. If the mentor is not skilled at challenging appropriately and is not protecting the protégé, challenging may lead to frustration and uncontrolled failure.

CHAPTER FIVE
DISCUSSION

This qualitative study explored the developmental interactions between Japanese sensei and key American leaders at Toyota Motor Manufacturing Kentucky (TMMK) in the three years following the initial hiring in 1986. By understanding the characteristics of these interactions and following the development of these relationships through the four phases of the mentoring relationship: initiation, cultivation, separation, and redefinition (Bullis & Bach, 1989; Kram, 1983), the study identified crucial mentor-mentee interactions as they relate to the Toyota Production System (TPS), scientific management, and quality management theory.

The first two phases of mentoring, initiation and cultivation, shaped the focus of this study. Understanding how Toyota's senseis initiated and cultivated the relationships with their American protégés is more relevant to organizational transformation in comparison to the separation and redefinition phases. Separation and redefinition phases are generally marked with the mentor and/or protégé exiting the organization or workgroup. Once the separation phase occurs, the work of the mentoring relationship is essentially finished and the relationship is reassessed. Therefore, the focus of this study has been on better understanding the initiation and cultivation phases of the relationship.

In this chapter I provide a discussion of the major findings related to the initiation and cultivation phases of the mentoring relationship. I also highlight the implications of these findings for organizations implementing TPS and then present several areas for possible future research and a brief summary of the research.

Research Questions

The two research questions that formed the basis of this study were:

1. What are the characteristics of the developmental relationship between early leaders at TMMK and their Japanese counterparts? This research question attempted to identify the most prominent relationship characteristics of the mentoring relationship at Toyota, including demographics, behaviors within the relationship, perceptions of knowledge, schedule of interactions, positive/negative experiences, and degrees of trust (D'Abate et al., 2003).

2. What are the common steps for early American leaders transitioning from the initiation phase to the cultivation phase of the mentoring relationship? Results addressing this question add to the significance of this study, given that the turning point from initiation to cultivation within a mentor relationship is not well developed in the literature.

I addressed these questions through an analysis of over a hundred stories provided by the study's seven participants.

The analysis sheds considerable light on the characteristics and experiences within the mentoring relationships during the early years of Toyota at Georgetown. The results drew attention to a framework that was located in the initiation to cultivation phases and provide specific information about how the Japanese at Toyota were able to transplant TPS within an American culture. Findings highlighted that the Japanese did this by instilling quality management thinking into protégés and by using PDCA (Plan, Do, Check, Act) cycles of improvement. I refer to these two aspects of the Japanese mentoring processes as the *Path to Self-Learning Quality Management* (PSLQM).

The Path to Self-Learning

PSLQM provides the formulation for the model seen in Figure 11. This model overlays Kram's (1983) first two phases of mentoring (initiation and cultivation) with the processes that the sensei-protégé relationships followed. The PSLQM model shown in Figure 11 also adds to Figure 10 on page 100 above "Scientific Management Application" in the initiation phase and "Quality Management Learning" in the cultivation phase. Initiation included learning to see, listening, and perfecting the standard. Once the standard was perfected, the senseis expected the Americans to solve problems using PDCA methodology. Senseis continued to challenge their protégés in order to both advance and understand their thinking through the application of PDCA and challenging assignments. Senseis used questioning to determine if the protégé's thinking was advancing beyond the specific problem to the stage of self-learning.

Figure 11
Path to Self-Learning Quality Management Model

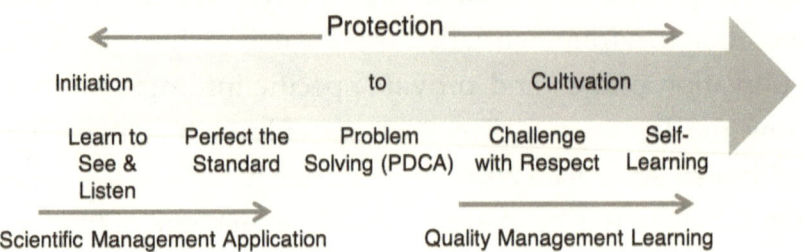

Kram (1983) describes the initiation phase as a "period of six months to a year during which time the relationship started and begins to have importance to both" mentor and protégé (p. 622). During this time, fantasies become expectations, those expectations are met, and there are opportunities for interaction (including technical assistance, challenging work, coaching, and so forth) around work tasks. The PSLQM demonstrates the application of Scientific Management by learning to see, perfecting the standard work tasks, and learning how to solve problems within that work under the guidance of a mentor. In the PSLQM the mentor, protégé, and the actual work tasks are all linked to both improve the work and teach the protégé to learn the standard and then improve the standard through scientific management.

Kram (1983) describes the cultivation phase as a "period of two to five years during which time the range of career and psychosocial functions expand to a maximum" (p. 622). Kram describes how both individuals benefit from the relationship, opportunities increase for meaningful interaction, and emotional bond increases. More specifically, the PSLQM demonstrates how the mentor teaches quality management thinking through the application of PDCA, problem solving, and challenging assignments. Additionally, the mentor validates this thinking through constant questioning and challenging assignments. The mentor continues to improve the work and the organization through the protégé, constantly questioning them, until the protégé begins to think differently and apply quality management beyond the task at hand. The PSLQM demonstrates how the mentor cannot only instill quality management thinking into the protégé but also validate that the protégé is learned how to apply quality management on an ongoing basis.

Characteristics of the Sensei Relationship

The first research question led to the identification of the characteristics associated with mentoring relationships at Toyota. Table 12 shows the characteristics found via the literature review as well as additional characteristics found via analyzing the interviews. The research specifically brought the following additional characteristics for the initiation phase to light: areas of expertise, protection, and teaching/learning standards. The additional characteristics found for the cultivation phase include mutual protection, problem solving skills, and challenging assignments to confirm the occurrence of transformative learning.

Table 12

Mentoring Characteristics

Phases of Mentoring	Characteristics Kram (1983) and Haines (2003)	Additional Characteristics from Research
Initiation	Mutual interests defined Task-centered relationship Invitation extended	Areas of Expertise Defined Protection Teaching/Learning Standards
Cultivation	Frequent and meaningful interactions Strong professional and personal relationship Transformative learning occurs Highly productive relationship Mutual growth	Mutual Protection Applying problem solving skills beyond the problems at hand Challenging Assignments to check that transformative learning is occurring

Note. Kram, K. (1983). Phases of the mentor relationship. *Academy of Management Journal*, 26(4), 608–625. doi.org/10.2307/255910 and Haines, S. (2003). The Mentor-protégé relationship. *American Journal of Pharmaceutical Education*, 67(82), 458–464.

I have summarized the key characteristics and demographics for early dedicated, formal sensei relationships at Toyota as follows:

1. Protégés did not directly report to their sensei, rather the formal relationship was outside of the normal organizational structure and may have led to increased success of the relationship.
2. Senseis seemed to be the same age as the American managers, while those for the American group leaders were older.

3. Senseis had more technical and TPS knowledge and experience than the Americans but less knowledge and experience in managing an American workforce.
4. The duration of the developmental relationship between an American and his Japanese counterpart was short-term for some and long-term for others.
5. Mentor-protégé interactions were normally one-to-one and were both regularly scheduled and unscheduled.
6. The medium of interaction was face-to-face.
7. Although the mentor-protégé interactions were primarily dyadic, group interactions were common and sometimes included more than one sensei.
8. The direction of most relationships was at the same organizational level, except for the General Manager, who reported directly to President Cho.
9. All interactions were between Toyota senseis and the Americans, primarily at Georgetown.
10. The purposes of these interactions were both work-related and developmental.
11. The interactions were both focused on short-term performance and long-term development.
12. The degree of structure of the interactions was informal and unstructured.
13. There was no overall development coordinator but there was a Senior Executive Coordinator who seemed directly involved with the Japanese

but not with the Americans.
14. The choice to participate in these relationships was mandatory for both the Japanese and the Americans.
15. Each relationship with between a sensei and an American was assigned and began upon hiring.
16. The participants indicated that the senseis seemed to have been provided with some preparation or training beforehand, but the nature and extent of that preparation was unknown.

Additional characteristics shown in Table 12 for the initiation phase of the mentor relationship include areas of expertise, protection, and teaching and learning standards. For the cultivation phase, additional characteristics are mutual protection, applying problem solving skills beyond the problems at hand, and challenging assignments to check for transformative learning. It is important to note that mentors may or may not have more knowledge in certain areas important to the relationship—in this case the protégés had more knowledge of how to work with a U.S. workforce. It is important to identify these areas of expertise so that mutual benefit may occur leading into the cultivation phase. Protection, problem solving, and challenging assignments will be discussed in the following sections.

The Theme of Protection

Although Bright (2005) has identified protection as one of many terms associated with the senpai-kohai relationship (historical Japanese senior-junior mentor-protégé relationship), perhaps the most striking research finding of this study is the extent to which protection was central to the mentoring relationships in the early days at Toyota Georgetown. Notably, both the sepia-kohai relationship characteristic of organizational mentoring in Japan and the oyabun-kobun (leader-subordinate) relationship characteristic of apprenticeships are distinguished by "protection" (Bright, 2005). Protégés perceive that organizations with formal mentoring programs value their wellbeing, strongly consider their goals and values, take pride in their work accomplishments, and show concern for them (Park et al., 2016). Therefore, protection from potential negative experiences becomes another positive experience for the protégé, thereby reinforcing in his or her mind the positive assessment of the organization.

As an organization attempts to emulate a production system similar to Toyota's, the first obvious lesson prescribes the foundational need and importance of establishing mentor/protégé relationships at multiple organizational levels. Once established, the organization should consider applying the lessons highlighted below, which come from the stories listed in Table 11 of the previous chapter:

1. As a mentor, be prepared to calm your mentee in stressful situations. Calming may involve actually removing them from the situation.
2. Anyone may become emotional with or without facts. Always deal with facts, but, recognize others may not. Agree with other mentors to protect mentees from negative emotional experiences, particularly in times of high stress.
3. Coach participants on what may cause difficult

emotional experiences and prepare them accordingly.
4. If you are providing adequate amounts of protection, don't be surprised if your mentee protects in turn.
5. Executive Leaders must determine how the elements of a complex system operate together. They must be seen to be leading the systematic approach. If your protégé is an executive leader, protect them from representing or becoming identified with only one element of the systematic approach.
6. Create an environment where failure is OK, and, while protecting your mentee from failure, don't eliminate future opportunities to learn from failure. Note this may take different forms in different situations.

As shown in Table 11 and Figure 11, protection is found throughout the initiation and cultivation phases of the relationship. Protection is important in the initiation phase because problems will inevitably occur when protégés are learning and perfecting the standard. Initially, senseis are teaching protégés the proper response to problems, which involves problem recognition and solution using PDCA. Note, this is very different than some corporate cultures of cover-up and blame, which is one reason why the mentor-protégé relationship is critical in implementing TPS. Working within the TPS, protégés must be able to see and recognize problems in order to respond to them appropriately by applying PDCA. Again, PDCA is making a plan to solve problems, doing that plan, checking to see if that plan worked, and adjusting the plan for further problem solving. In order for that transformation to occur naturally and continuously, problems must not only be discussed or thought of as failures. They must be treated as opportunities to improve. However, depending on facts and perceptions around the problem, others may react inappropriately and emotionally. Protecting protégés from these responses is necessary to continually apply PDCA and advance to the cultivation phase of the relationship. In this way the success of the mentor depends upon the success of the protégé and the success of the protégé depends on the success of the mentor/protégé relationship.

In the cultivation phase, protection also occurs but at a different, more sophisticated level. At times, it's even mutual. As protégés move from learning and following standards to applying PDCA and thus making their own improvements to those standards, conflicts can surface, as not every improvement will be successful. In fact, some may cause further problems. Similarly, the result of challenging assignments may end in failure, which also increases the likelihood of conflict and the expression of negative emotions. As interviewees noted, removing emotion, focusing on facts, and applying the same style of questions to understand why the expected results were or weren't achieved remains critical to both understanding how the protégé is thinking as well as providing protection. This process of questioning allows for transparency in moving protégés to a new level of self-thinking through the now more natural application of PDCA whenever possible.

Scientific Management Application and Quality Management Learning

The final research question directed the research toward identifying the common steps characteristic of the transition from the initiation phase to the cultivation phase as it occurred at Toyota Georgetown. Those steps were: learn to see and listen, perfect the standard, and solve problems using PDCA. The initiation phase, which includes perfecting and improving the standard, aligns with the application of scientific management theory.

Engineer the Product and Process

Taylorism or scientific management (Tompkins, 2005) recognizes the need to reduce organizational complexity through standardization. Taylor accomplished this by dividing work into defined tasks and determining the one best way to do the work. Additionally, he measured performance and offered economic incentives. With everyone focused on the one best way, organizations could improve socioeconomic conditions by eliminating waste and increasing profits. Scientific management includes right place/time/tools/materials, written work instructions, time studies to understand each task, and incentives. Toyota in 1986 had already developed robust standards for the new U.S. workers to learn and perfect.

So, the first part of the mentor relationship was to observe the standard then perfect the standard. For an organization to apply the same type of process Toyota used during the Georgetown ramp-up, they must first engineer the product and process simultaneously. Figure 12 adds "Engineer the Product and Process" to Figure 11 to show that engineering the product and process comes prior to the initiation phase of the mentor relationship and is a pre-requisite for both initiation and cultivation.

Figure 12
Engineer the Standard and Develop Standards

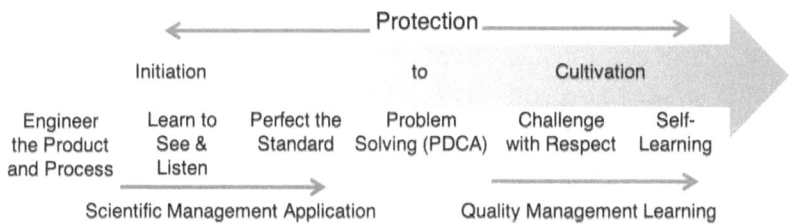

Rodger Lewis, in his interview, noted Toyota's engineering as an ah-ha moment:

> The primary learning from Toyota is very proactive versus reactive. The auto industry I was familiar with was very reactive, whereas Toyota is very proactive. Toyota is looking to confirm their strategy. They're not trying to just identify problems after the fact. Toyota knows what the outcomes are going to be, and the process (i.e. the standard) is designed to confirm that they designed the product and process appropriately. In other auto industries you are kind of dealing with it on a 'we've got a problem, let's fix it', in more of a reactive sense. Then, the company needs to change the engineering and the drawings to fix the problems. Therefore, the major difference between Toyota and other auto companies is that we

never issued re-works at Toyota. We maintained the standard. At other companies, they would modify the drawing, issue re-works, and issue engineering changes. That never happened at Toyota.

Lewis' "ah-ha" moment was when he realized that Toyota engineered the product and process simultaneously, whereas other auto companies did not. Toyota then trained team members to the engineered process to also meet the specifications of the engineered product. Tools like *andon* (a signal for help) were introduced so team members could alert leaders when the standard was not met as quickly as possible. More importantly, Toyota created checks (e.g. quality and production verifications) that confirmed their strategy of both product and process design throughout the production of the automobile.

Toyota had newly hired members watch and see the standard before they performed job functions. They had newly hired U.S. personnel perfect the standard before they could make an improvement. Then, and only then, could the workforce improve the process with one caveat: the process could be improved but the product would most likely not be reengineered. Lewis also noted that the process was designed to operate under total capacity to give the opportunity to improve the process. Leaders were taught to manage above the capacity and to challenging the workforce to improve. The forethought into engineering cars, the process, as well as the actual procedure to improve the process, was extraordinary during a critical time in Toyota's history as it established U.S. operations.

The Continual Search for Quality

The results of this study indicate that the transition from the initiation phase to the cultivation phase aligns with quality management theory. Quality management theory from the 1950s built upon scientific management and statistical process control (SPC). SPC, as opposed to quality control by end product or service inspection, involves collecting data at different steps in the production process to meet a standard (i.e., specification) and thereby eliminate causes of variation and assure quality of the end product or service. The Plan-Do-Check-Act cycle, which Deming introduced to Japan, was used to implement a continuous improvement modality to immediate work processes. It is clear that the senseis attempted to systematically instill PDCA-thinking into their protégés (Tompkins, 2005).

Additionally, Deming's philosophy went far beyond statistical process control and included the driving out of fear, the routinization of constant improvement, instituting training and leadership, taking action towards transformation, and instituting programs that lead to self-improvement (Tompkins, 2005). Through the protection and trust exhibited within the mentor relationships at Toyota, it's clear the senseis institutionalized leadership, led constant improvement, and facilitated self-learning through the mentor process. As total quality management (TQM) was becoming a fad in U.S. companies in the 1980s and 1990s, Toyota had already established a systematic approach in utilizing mentors to engrain TQM thinking into the fabric of the organization. Japan moved TQM from a fad to culture.

As outlined by Kram (1983), the following took place during the cultivation phases of the sensei-protégé relationships at Toyota: both individuals benefited from the increasingly productive relationship and opportunities for more meaningful interaction increased, which resulted in more transformational learning. Therefore, the concepts of transactional and transformational learning were added to the model in Figure 13. Transactional learning occurs during the period of learning the standards and then applying PDCA at the individual problem level. Transformational learning occurs when protégés learn quality management techniques and apply them beyond the problem at hand. Thus, protégé learning starts at PDCA and continues through self-learning. The overlap in the problem solving (PDCA) and challenge with respect areas, stems from the iterative process that occurs between the mentor and protégé until the protégé enters the point of self-learning.

Figure 13
Full Self-Learning Quality Management Model

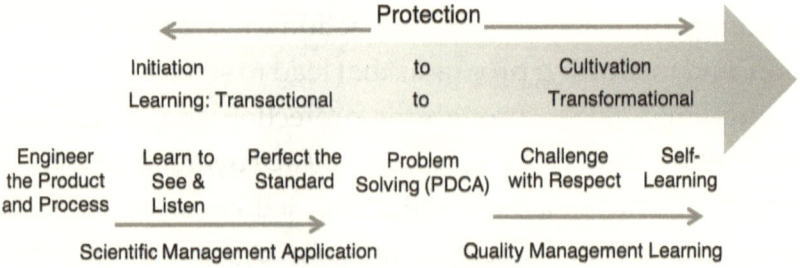

In summary, the Process to Self-Learning model incorporates Kram's (1983) first two phases of the mentor relationship (initiation and cultivation); the process Toyota established for the newly hired U.S. workforce (learn to see and listen, perfect the standard, solve problems, challenge with respect, and self-learning); scientific management and quality management (including developing a standard to apply scientific management); the concept of protection built from within the mentor relationship; as well as differentiating transactional and transformational learning. Within this model, the transition from initiation to cultivation takes place in terms of the turning point from transactional to transformational learning.

Transformational Learning

Embedding quality management thinking beyond solving the problem at hand (transformational learning) seemed to signal the mentor/protégé relationship transitioning to the cultivation phase. The Japanese coordinators challenged Americans to a point of self-learning, starting with problem solving and then adding other challenges. These challenges and problem-solving events were at times transactional and eventually transformational as demonstrated in Figure 13 above. The turning points from initiation to cultivation take place during the turning point from transactional quality improvement to transformational quality improvement. I summarize observations clarifying this perspective as follows:

1. As Russ learned from Mr. Cho, when problems are solved or when challenging assignments

are implemented, improvements must always be compared to the standard (the current one best way things are done as well as the results of that one best way). This is in order to determine if there were actually an improvement and the thinking that went into the improvement as well as the thinking post-implementation. When this happens, leaders can ask the most appropriate questions to check on the status of the protégé's actual learning of quality management. When the protégé presents the results in a fashion that implies they already asked themselves the same reflective questions the mentor would ask, it is a sign that transformational learning may have occurred.

2. As Jeff says, bad news comes first, last, and always, because discussions must be around challenges—what did not work and why—to enable further improvement. The strength of the relationship is essential, and protection builds trust and trust allows for questioning of this nature. This proved difficult for some Americans. This highlights the importance of protection, especially during the early phases of the relationship, and builds trust, which enables transformational learning to occur. When protection and trust are in play, and the protégé routinely discusses what did not work and why, transformational learning may have occurred.

3. As David says, the emphasis is on the word *learning*, as in learning by doing. The point of

a mentor challenging a protégé within a TPS environment is to help the mentee become a self-learner of quality management outside of the mentor-mentee relationship. When the protégé begins to apply learning outside the problem at hand, transformational learning may have occurred.
4. Additionally, as David reflected, when making an improvement, regardless of whether the mentee meets, falls short of, or exceeds the target, the same questions must be asked because the outcome was almost by definition not the expected outcome. The mentor must ask the right questions so the mentee can better self-reflect on future challenges. This teaches the mentee how to apply quality management in any scenario. When the protégé is prepared for the questioning and begins to apply the same type of questioning to other problems, transformational learning may have occurred.

The primary lessons learned regarding the transition to the cultivation phase of the mentoring process focuses exclusively on understanding the thinking of the mentee. That is, understanding if they were applying quality management thinking. To this end, the process of moving the mentee to self-learning can be improved by understanding the following:

1. Learn how to ask the right questions but do not give the answer.
2. Create an environment of mutual trust and

respect so everyone can focus on achieving perfection, though perfection will never be achieved.
3. Learn by doing. Create an environment where self-learning of quality management techniques can occur.
4. Ask questions to determine the extent to which self-learning is taking place, validating the understanding of the protégé.
5. Always compare the improvements to the standard to see if improvement actually occurred. This will help formulate the questions to challenge the protégé.
6. Whether or not the target is met, missed, or exceeded, ask the same questions to determine how thinking can be improved next time. This helps remove emotion and keeps the focus on quality management.
7. Bad news comes first, last, and always, so that individuals and teams can learn how to not repeat mistakes and improve their thinking. Again, this removes emotion and keeps protégés and mentors focused on quality management initiatives through continual PDCA.

The turning point to cultivation does not appear to be a single event but rather a spiraling loop of questioning and challenging assignments until the mentor enters transformational learning. The concept of *liminal space,* defined as a "transformative stage in the learning process in which the learner begins to reframe or experience a shift in their understanding," may help explain the shift from initiation to cultivation (Bishop, 2018, p. 11). In the space between initiation and cultivation, the mentor may continue the iterative looping until the sensei validates that the protégé is indeed in a phase of self-learning of quality management. Additionally, the mentor may have to continually reinforce self-learning within the cultivation phase in order to instill the PDCA-mindset into the protégé.

Senseis strive for perfection but understand that both they and the protégés will fall short of perfection with each iterative improvement cycle. In order to continually improve operationally, and to develop the protégé simultaneously, the mentor gives the protégé challenging assignments. A turning point is when the protégé begins to discover challenging assignments based on operational needs. After each challenging assignment or problem-solving engagement, the mentor asks questions comparing the results to the standard, thereby checking the validity of the improvement and the protégé's thinking process behind the improvement, the protégé's interpretation of the results, and the next way ahead.

The protégé experiences a significant turning point when they begin to ask themselves the same type of questions they would be receiving from their mentor. For this to take hold organizationally, the relationship must be within the context of a *learning organization* or under senior management attempting to build such an organization. A learning organization, defined by Senge (1994) is an organization "where people continually expand their capacity to create the results they truly desire, where new and expansive patterns of thinking are nurtured, where collective aspiration is set free, and where people are continually learning how to learn together" (p. 1).

Once the protégé has begun to apply this type of PDCA thinking to each and every scenario, it becomes more and more obvious to the mentor that the protégé has had a turning point and is able to continually self-learn quality management techniques in other scenarios. Table 13 below summarizes this loop and turning points to quality management thinking within the cultivation phase of the mentor relationship.

Table 13
Turning Points to Quality Management

Sensei-Protégé Loop to Cultivation	Protégé Transformative Quality Management Learning
Mentor aims for perfection.	Protégé aims for perfection.
Mentor gives challenging assignments based on the gaps in protégé's thinking and operational improvements needed.	Protégé finds challenging assignments based on operational needs.
Mentor understands the thinking and actual results behind the improvement by comparing improvements to the standard.	Protégé compares the implemented improvements to the standard and the expected results to improve their own thinking for later improvements.

Limitations and Future Research

This study was limited by interviewing only a small number of Americans hired to Toyota between 1986 and 1992. With snowball sampling, an attempt was made to reach out to as many as possible, but some were unable to be contacted, were not available, or were deceased. The participants included some of the very few initial hires to management and two of the initial group of 26 group leaders. To draw further insights into the process that Toyota followed for mentor-protégé relationships it may help to conduct interviews of the Japanese coordinators and executive coordinators who worked during the first three years of Toyota Georgetown. Japanese individuals were not offered as potential participants during snowball sampling. These individuals might add insight for answering additional research questions such as "Was Japanese protection of the Americans pre-planned, and if so, how?" Possible future research documents are offered in Appendices D, E, F, H, and I.

Summary

The purpose of this study was to understand characteristics of the developmental interactions between Japanese senseis and early American leaders at Toyota Motor Manufacturing Kentucky during the late 1980s and early 1990s as they relate to the initial two phases of mentoring set forth by Kram (1983): initiation and cultivation. This research has shown how the initiation phase of the mentor relationships was characterized by learning to see, learning to listen, perfecting the standard, and the beginnings of problem solving. As discussed in this chapter, a specific set of behaviors facilitated the movement of the mentees from the initiation phase to the cultivation stage, which included the mentor protecting the protégé, challenging the protégé for problem solving via PDCA, giving the protégé challenging assignments, and constantly questioning to check on the protégé's progress with quality management learning. Throughout, self-learning was the ultimate point of the cultivation phase.

This study is unique in that it involved only those Americans who were engaged in mentoring relationships in the early days of Toyota Georgetown. It included individuals who were mentored by the Japanese and who were, at the same time, responsible for mentoring other Americans. Americans were interacting with the best Japanese senseis during a crucial moment in time for what became one of the world's largest automotive companies.

The major takeaways are that mentor-like relationships are critical in a TPS-like transformation. First, leaders must ensure that the organization actually has standards in place. Workers can be taught the one best way on how to perform the work following scientific management principles. Next, there must be an approach to protect individuals in the form of mentor relationships from traditional emotional responses to problems and stressful situations. Having transparency and a clearly defined problem-solving approach, rather than the typical American response of blaming and finger pointing would help build the trust needed to apply PDCA techniques. Then, as protection continues, the senseis must continually give challenging assignments and question results compared to the standard to test the learning of protégés and teach them how to self-apply quality management thinking.

Attempts to emulate Toyota have been made throughout the United States by restructuring work, reengineering processes, and attempting to do more with less. Those who have applied Toyota's unique approach to quality management, without applying the robust engineering and scientific management application may also find failure. These efforts started as fads in the mid to late 20th century and continue today. U.S. industries have adopted aspects of TPS without understanding how mentoring, Japanese management systems, and the unique Toyota approach impact how employees learn and apply that learning beyond the problem at hand. This focus on only one element of TPS—restricting work into a lean format—while ignoring another vital elements of TPS—a culture of mutual trust and respect between employees, management, and the community—provides a likely explanation as to why so many efforts to integrate TPS into American firms has failed.

While total quality management initiatives, such as TPS, have been implemented in other settings with limited success (Cameron & Quinn, 2011), the findings from this study may help improve implementation successes in other organizations. As leaders in those organizations adapt Toyota-style production, leadership, and management systems, they should consider using mentors, ensure the protection of protégés, use scientific management techniques to develop and teach the "one best way," and use quality management theory to instill a Plan-Do-Check-Act mindset into protégés. When protégés cross the threshold of applying quality management into transformational self-learning, they may soon be ready to mentor others within a TPS-like system.

The House of TPS

Many exciting stories were told by participants throughout my study. The one that stands out most dramatically is Russ's story about what we believe to be the first House of Toyota to appear in the United States circa 1989. This story was briefly told in the context of "Protection," as Mr. Cho insisted that Russ be seen as the leader of TPS not TPM. This story demonstrates how Toyota started Total Preventative Maintenance in the Power Train Division, identifies Catesby Prewitt as the first American group leader hired at Georgetown Toyota, and describes how Russ developed the House to convince Mr. Cho to implement TPM at Toyota.

*****

Russ Scaffede was hired as the first General Manager and later Vice President of Toyota's Powertrain division in 1988. Catesby Prewitt, the maintenance manager at Toyota Powertrain, was hired by Russ from the manufacturing division of Toyota. Eventually the duo would implement TPM for Toyota. The following presents Russ's story in his own words as told to me during participant interviews but has been edited for clarity.

The story of TPM at Toyota Powertrain starts when Art Smalley, who lived and worked in Japan, when he asked me to come to Japan in 1988 or 1989 during the beginning stages of Toyota Powertrain. I was aware that Toyota was teaching all the elements of the Toyota Production System, but they were not implementing preventative maintenance, despite relying on only one machine. Toyota was teaching quality checks, quick tool changes, those things. I understood that with only one piece of equipment, it was especially important to keep it up and running in a preventative sense.

While in Japan, Art and I discussed two books written in Kanji (Japanese language), which could be found on every desk at Toyota: *The Implementation of TPM*, and *Training of TPM*. I didn't know what they were at the time, but pretty soon I'm in this big meeting with a gentleman named Tom Harada, head of Kamigo manufacturing engineering. Tom was well known because he helped start the famous Kamigo engine plant where Taiichi Ohno was the original plant manager. I was asked to read English translations of the two books, each with an introduction by Director Kusonoki.

My first reaction was "Oh great! They brought me all the way over here to Japan and they want me to read this stupid book just because Kusonoki wrote the introduction."

However, after beginning to read the books on the long plane ride home, I realized TPM was exactly what the power train division needed. The books clearly outlined the initial two steps: first, the leader of the facility (which was me) pulls together a steering committee and, second, that team establishes a 3-year implementation plan.

So, I got home and continued reading for a week or so 'til I got both finished. Finally, I went to work and was going to call my first TPM steering committee meeting. So, I called Bud Sato, Wayne Ripberger, Catesby Prewitt, a couple of the coordinators, group leaders from maintenance and production and set up my first steering committee meeting.

Well, that night, apparently faxes went back and forth over the ocean like crazy, and the next day Bud came running up and said, "Russ-son, Russ-son, Russ-son, you can't do TPM. Director Hayakawa [the head of all powertrain] said, you can't do TPM."

I said, "Wait a minute, you guys gave me the books in Japan. What do you mean I can't do TPM?"

"You can't do TPM."

I said, "But it's what we need here. We got to do TPM."

Well, the next thing I know I've been asked that I go see Mr. Cho. So, I go to Mr. Cho and he says, "I hear you want to put TPM in?"

And I said, "I really do, Mr. Cho. You guys are trained in everything, but I don't understand it. You're not training preventative maintenance."

Mr. Cho said, "Well, what I'm going to do is I'm going to send you to Japan for a week, but your job when you come back, Russ-son, you must show me where TPM fits into TPS, number one. Number two, if I let you do this, you must still be seen as the person representing TPS. You cannot lead a TPM steering committee. Wayne or Catesby can, but you can't."

So, I went back to Japan for a week. Like they always do, the Japanese had the entire trip set up and pre-planned. The first meeting is with Director Hayakawa. What I find out was, as Art later told me, I was the guinea pig. Tom Harada wanted to put this in. He felt the younger guys hiring into Toyota weren't that mechanically inclined, like the folks who have been at Toyota for many years. So therefore, he felt they needed TPM. However, Director Hayakawa, who had been there for thirty something years, thought it would be a waste of money and time to do it, and he wasn't letting Tom do it. So they were going to send me back home to try to do it in the United States.

So, I go into a meeting with Director Hayakawa and an interpreter, and this was the actual conversation. I mean, Director Hayakawa had only been in the United States once and he spoke very, very little English.

So he says through his interpreter, "I hear you want to put in TPM?"

And I said, "Yes, Director, we need to put in TPM because the American team members need to be taught how to maintain this equipment, do preventative maintenance."

He said, "This is one of the dumbest conversations I've ever had. Everybody knows that everybody in a plant is involved in preventative maintenance of the equipment."

I said, "Director Hayakawa, you don't understand the United States. Not only do we not have everybody involved in TPM, many of these people come from industries where because of skilled trades and stuff, they're forbidden to do preventative maintenance."

"Russ-son, I've never heard anything so stupid. Anybody knows you would not start your lawnmower without checking the oil in the lawnmower. You would not send your wife and kids out in the car without checking the air in the tires, understanding the oil and the water in the car, the fan belt in the car. You wouldn't do that."

I said, "Director Hayakawa, I know we wouldn't do that, but in our factories, we do not have our team members doing that and they've never been trained to."

Back home, we thought it was really stupid to assume

that someone hiring into a company would automatically know you got to maintain the equipment, but that's what they expected in Japan. A new hire would be trained by fellow team members and leaders how to change oil, how to check limit switch. So, they put me on a four-day visit to four plants that had won the Japan Institute of Plant Maintenance Award. So, you've got to understand TPM comes out of the Japan Institute of Plant Maintenance.

But even though Toyota is one of the biggest funders of the institute, Toyota does not practice TPM in their factories. They took me to four places, and it was very clear what they were trying to show me.

The uniqueness of the Toyota guys is they're never going to tell you, "No." They're going to have you come to that conclusion on your own. So we toured these factories and it was clear they didn't have kanban, they didn't have the 5S. There was a lot of things missing that helped make the Toyota Production System what it is.

On the way home I drew a house with the pillars I'm talking about and I had TPM as the bedrock base. And then I had a sun—at the time I had arrows coming out of the sun—and I listed the tools: the Toyota Kaizen, standardized work, 5S such and such. And I got home, and I got this thing drawn up.

And I went and I showed it to Mr. Cho, and I said, "So here's where TPM, this bedrock, fits into TPS. I said, if machines start breaking down, and this is our bedrock, I swear, Mr. Cho, at some point we start losing the rest of TPS. We can't afford to have things break down."

Well, I'll never forget it. I don't know what he thinks today. I'm sure he would attest that he said it, and he said,

"Russ-son...This is the most perfect example of the Toyota Production System I've ever seen."

Now, whether or not he believed that from the heart, I've cherished it ever since and I've never let it go. And he said, "I understand what you're saying. I'm going to let you put in TPM, but remember what I said, you must stand for TPS. You cannot be seen as representing TPM."

We then started on our TPM journey. And ever since then, I've used the House that came out of that TPM initiative. I absolutely believe and Steve has done the research to justify that this is the first house ever in the United States. Again, it was 1988. The house traveled around the country and has taken many forms since then, because when you work for Toyota, you got to go out and give talks, be committed to helping others. Since then, houses have cropped up all over in all kinds of forms.

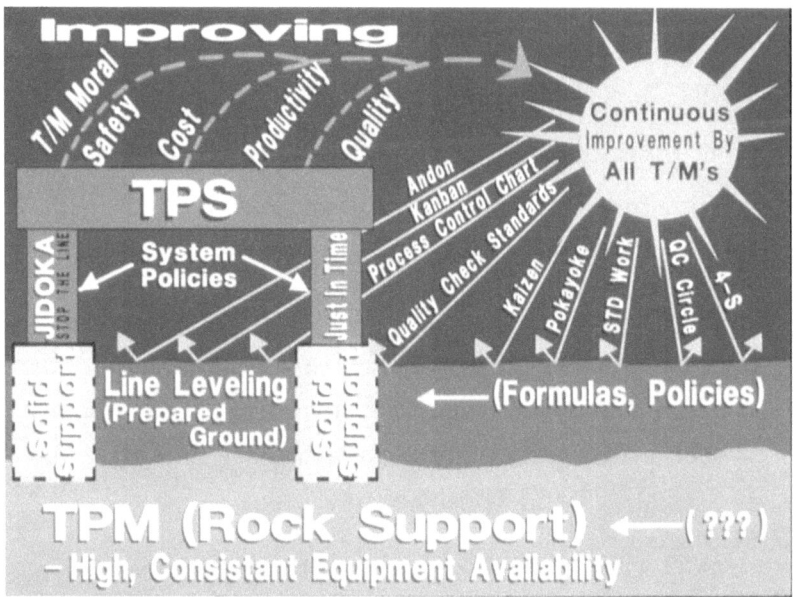

The first house of TPS by Russ Scaffede

REFERENCES

Aaker, D. A. (1994). Building a brand: The Saturn story. *California Management Review, 36*(2), 114–133.

Alisic, S., Boet, S., Sutherland, S., & Bould, M. D. (2016). A qualitative study exploring mentorship in anesthesiology: Perspectives from both sides of the relationship. *Canadian Journal of Anesthesia/Journal Canadien Danesthésie, 63*(7), 851–861. doi.org/10.1007/s12630-016-0649-3

Allen, M. (Ed.) (2017). *The Sage encyclopedia of communication research methods* (Vols. 1–4). Sage.

Allen, T. D., Eby, L. T., & Lentz, E. (2006). Mentorship behaviors and mentorship quality associated with formal mentoring programs: Closing the gap between research and practice. *Journal of Applied Psychology, 91*(3), 567–578. doi: 10.1037/0021-9010.91.3.567

Aoki, K. (2015). Labour Relations and HRM in the automotive industry. In Nieuwenhuis, P. & Wells, P. (Eds.), *The Global Automotive Industry* (pp. 83-94). John Wiley & Sons.

Bishop, N. E. (2018). *Exploring the impact of feedback on learning transfer in the liminal space for information literacy.* (Unpublished doctoral dissertation). ProQuest Dissertations and Theses.

Bowers, D. G., & Seashore, S. E. (1966). Predicting organizational effectiveness with a four-actor theory of leadership. *Administrative Science Quarterly, 11*(2), 238–63. doi.org/10.2307/2391247

Bright, M. L. (2005). Can Japanese mentoring enhance understanding of Western mentoring? *Employee Relations, 27*(4), 325–339. doi:10.1108/01425450510605679

Bullis, C., & Bach, B. W. (1989). Are mentor relationships helping organizations? An exploration of developing mentee-mentor-organizational identifications using turning point analysis. *Communication Quarterly, 37*(3), 199–213. doi.org/10.1080/01463378909385540

Burns, M. B. (2004). *Transforming leadership.* Grove.

Cameron, K. S., & Quinn, R. E. (2011). *Diagnosing and changing organizational culture: Based on the competing values framework.* Wiley.

Cars that made history (2019). http://www.cars-history.org

Chappell, L. (2007). In Georgetown, Toyota became global. *Automotive News.* https://www.autonews.com/article/20071029/ANA03/710290319/in-georgetown-toyota-became-global

Chun, J., Sosik, J., & Yun, N. (2012). A longitudinal study of mentor and protégé outcomes in formal mentoring relationships. *Journal of Organizational Behavior, 33*(8), 1071–1094. doi.org/10.1002/job.1781

Coghlan, D., & Brydon-Miller, M. (Eds.). (2014). *The SAGE encyclopedia of action research* (Vols. 1-2). Sage.

Company History (n.d.). https://pressroom.toyota.com/company-history/

D'Abate, C. (2010). Developmental interactions for business students: Do they make a difference? *Journal of Leadership & Organizational Studies, 17*(2), 143–155. doi.org/10.1177/1548051810370795

D'Abate, C., Eddy, E., & Tannenbaum, S. (2003). What's in a name? A literature-based approach to understanding mentoring, coaching, and other constructs that describe developmental interactions. *Human Resource Development Review, 2*(4), 360–384. doi:10.1177/1534484303255033

DiMaggio, P. J., & Powell, W. W. (1983). The iron cage revisited: Institutional isomorphism and collective rationality in organizational fields. *The American Sociological Association, 48*(2), 147–160. ssrn.com/abstract=1504516

Dioso-Henson, L. (2012). The effect of reciprocal peer tutoring and non-reciprocal peer tutoring on the performance of students in college Physics. *Research in Education, 87*(1), 34–49. doi.org/10.7227/RIE.87.1.3

Dyer, J., & Nobeoka, K. (2000). Creating and managing a high performance knowledge-sharing network: The Toyota case. *Strategic Management Journal, 21*(3), 345–367. doi.org/10.1002/(SICI)1097-0266(200003)21:3<345::AID-SMJ96>3.0.CO;2-N

Eby, L., & Allen, T. (2002). Further investigation of protégés' negative mentoring experiences. *Group*

& *Organization Management, 27*(4), 456–479. doi. org/10.1177/1059601102238357

Emiliani, B. (2018). *The triumph of classical management over lean management: How the tradition prevails and what to do about it.* Cubic.

England, G. W. (1983). Japanese and American management: Theory Z and beyond. *Journal of International Business Studies, 14*(2), 131–142. doi.org/10.1057/palgrave.jibs.8490522

Finley, F., Ivanitskaya, L., Kennedy, M., & Hofmann, P. (2007). Mentoring junior healthcare administrators: A description of mentoring practices in 127 U.S. hospitals. *Journal of Healthcare Management, 52*(4), 260–269. doi:10.1097/00115514-200707000-00009

Freund, A. (2009). Oral history as process-generated data. *Historical Social Research, 34*(1), 22–48.

Fujimoto, T. (1999). *The evolution of a manufacturing system at Toyota.* Oxford University Press.

Glaser, B. G., & Strauss, A. L. (2017). *The discovery of grounded theory: Strategies for qualitative research.* Routledge.

Haines, S. (2003). The Mentor-Protégé relationship. *American Journal of Pharmaceutical Education, 67*(82), 458–464. pdfs.semanticscholar.org/2273/93ac221475f-36d15eb239f599accd70cf3a7.pdf

Hanson, K. (2007, September 1). Toyota's Long Beach roots. *Long Beach-Press Telegram.*

Hezlett, S. A. (2005). Protégés' learning in mentoring relationships: A review of the literature and an exploratory case study. *Advances in Developing Human Resources, 7*(4), 505–526. doi.org/10.1177/1523422305279686

High, S. (2019). The emotional fallout of deindustrialization in Detroit. *Labor: Studies in Working-Class History of the Americas, 16*(1), 127–149. doi:10.1215/15476715-7269362

History Editors. (2018). Automobile History. https://www.history.com/topics/inventions/automobiles

Holweg, M. (2007). The genealogy of lean production. *Journal of Operations Management, 25*(2), 420–437. doi.org/10.1016/j.jom.2006.04.001

Inkpen, A. (2005). Learning through alliances: General Motors and NUMMI. *California Management Review, 47*(4), 114–136. doi.org/10.2307/41166319

Institute for Healthcare Improvement. (2005). Going lean in health care. *Innovation Series White Paper.* Institute for Healthcare Improvement.

Jenkins, S. (2013). David Clutterbuck, Mentoring and coaching. *International Journal of Sports Science & Coaching, 8*(1), 139–254. doi.org/10.1260/1747-9541.8.1.139

Kaplan, G. S., Peterson, S. H., Ching, J. M., & Blackmore, C. C. (2014). Why lean doesn't work for everyone. *BJM Quality and Safety, 23*(12), 970–73. doi.org/10.1136/

bmjqs-2014-003248

Kato, I., & Smalley, A. (2010). *Toyota Kaizen methods: Six steps to improvement.* CRC Press.

Katz, R. L. (1955). Skills of an effective administrator. *Harvard Business Review, 33*(1), 33–42.

Klauss, R. (1981). Formalized mentor relationships for management and executive development programs in the federal government. *Public Administration Review, 41*(4), 489–496. doi: 10.2307/975712

Krafcik, J. F. (1988). Triumph of the lean production system. *Sloan Management Review, 30*(1), 41–52.

Kram, K. (1983). Phases of the mentor relationship. *Academy of Management Journal, 26*(4), 608–625. doi: 10.2307/255910

Liker, J., & Meier, D. (2005). *The Toyota fieldbook.* McGraw-Hill.

Liker, J. K., & Meier, D. (2007). *Toyota talent: Developing your people the Toyota way.* McGraw-Hill.

Liker, J., & Convis, G. (2011). *The Toyota way to lean leadership: Achieving and sustaining excellence through leadership development.* McGraw-Hill.

Marrelli, T. (2004). Why mentoring is important. *Home Health Care Management & Practice, 16*(2), 122–123.

McCann, T., & Johannessen, L. (2010). Mentoring matters. *The English Journal, 99*(4), 94–96. jstor.org/stable/27807175

Merriam, S. B., & Tisdell, E. J. (2016). *Qualitative research: A guide to design and implementation*. Jossey-Bass.

Mihut, M. L. (2014). The theory of paternalism and its consequences in Japanese companies. *Review of Economic Studies and Research Virgil Madgearu, 7*(1), 69–80.

Mishina, K. (1995). Toyota motor manufacturing, U.S.A, Inc. *Harvard Business Review*.

Mumford, M., Zaccaro, S., Harding, F., Jacobs, T., & Fleishman, E. (2000). Leadership skills for a changing world: Solving complex social problems. *The Leadership Quarterly, 11*(1), 11–35. doi.org/10.1016/S1048-9843(99)00041-7

Northouse, P. G. (2012). *Leadership: Theory and practice* (6th ed.). Sage.

Ortony, A., & Turner, T. J. (1990). What's basic about basic emotions? *Psychological Review, 97*(3), 315–331. doi: 10.1037/0033-295x.97.3.315

Ouchi, W. G. (1981). *Theory Z: How American business can meet the Japanese challenge*. Addison-Wesley.

Park, J., Newman, A., Zhang, L., Wu, C., & Hooke, A. (2016). Mentoring functions and turnover intention: The mediating role of perceived organizational support. *The International Journal of Human Resource Management, 27*(11), 1173–1191. doi.org/10.1080/0958 5192.2015.1062038

Patton, M. Q. (2014). *Qualitative research & evaluation methods: Integrating theory and practice* (4th ed.). Sage.

Riggs, T. (2015). *Gale encyclopedia of U.S. economic history* (2nd ed., Vol. 2). Gale.

Ritchie, D. A. (2014). *Doing oral history.* Oxford University Press.

Rosser, M. (2005). Mentoring from the top: CEO perspectives. *Advances in Developing Human Resources, 7*(4), 527–539. doi.org/10.1177/1523422305279685

Rubel, D. (2007). Accessing their voice from anywhere: Analysis of the legal issues surrounding the online use of oral histories. *Archival Issues, 31*(2), 171–187. jstor.org/stable/41102157

Senge, P. (1994). *The Fifth discipline fieldbook: Strategies and tools for building a learning organization.* Doubleday.

Sherman, J. (1994). *In the rings of Saturn.* Oxford University Press.

Shook, J. (2010). How to change a culture: Lessons from NUMMI. *MIT Sloan Management Review, 51*(2), 42–51.

Singh, R., Ragins, B. R., & Tharenou, P. (2009). Who gets a mentor? A longitudinal assessment of the rising star hypothesis. *Journal of Vocational Behavior, 74*(1), 11–17. doi:10.1016/j.jvb.2008.09.009

Spear, S., & Bowen, H. K. (1999). Decoding the DNA of the Toyota production system. *Harvard Business Review, 77*, 96–108.

Srivastava, S., & Jomon, M. (2013). Outcome linkage in formal & supervisory mentoring in a business organization. *Indian Journal of Industrial Relations,* 49(1), 82–96. jstor.org/stable/23509801

Sugimoto, C. (2012). Initiation, cultivation, separation and redefinition: Application of Kram's mentoring framework to doctoral education in information and library science. *Journal of Education for Library and Information Science, 53*(2), 98–114. jstor.org/stable/23249102

Sullivan, J. J. (1983). A critique of theory Z. *The Academy of Management Review, 8*(1), 132–142. doi.org/10.2307/257175

Takezawa, S., & Whitehill, A. M. (1981). *Work ways: Japan and America.* Japan Institute of Labour.

Tansey, M., & Raju, S. (2017). Pricing, concentration & public policy: The U.S. automobile market. *Journal of Policy Modeling, 39*(5), 762–774. doi:10.1016/j.jpolmod.2017.07.004

Tompkins, J. R. (2005). *Organization theory and public management.* Wadsworth.

Toussaint, J., & Gerard, R. (2010). *On the mend: Revolutionizing healthcare to save lives and transform the industry.* Lean Enterprise Institute.

Toyota. (2012, August 12). Toyota's TABC plant celebrates 40 years of manufacturing in California. https://corporatenews.pressroom.toyota.com/releases/toyota tabc plant celebrates 40 years manufacturing california.htm

Transform. (n.d.). In *The Merriam-Webster Dictionary, New Trade Paperback* (2019). Merriam-Webster.

Treece, J. B. (2013, October 15). 10 ways the 1973 oil embargo changed the industry. *Automotive News*.

Viator, R., & Pasewark, W. R. (2005). Mentorship separation tension in the accounting profession: The consequences of delayed structural separation. *Accounting, Organizations and Society, 30*(4), 371–387. doi.org/10.1016/j.aos.2004.03.003

Tsutsui, W. (1996). W. Edwards Deming and the origins of quality control in Japan. *Journal of Japanese Studies, 22*(2), 295-325. jstor.org/stable/132975

Vlasic, B. (2017, April 10). Toyota to invest $1.3 billion in Kentucky plant. *New York Times*.

Wang, S., Tomlinson, E. C., & Noe, R. A. (2010). The role of mentor trust and protégé internal locus of control in formal mentoring relationships. *Journal of Applied Psychology, 95*(2), 358–367. doi.org/10.1037/a0017663

Wendrich, W. (Ed.). (2016). *Archaeology and apprenticeship: Body knowledge, identity, and communities of practice.* University of Arizona Press.

Wilms, W. W. (1996). *Restoring prosperity: How workers and managers are forging a new culture of cooperation.* Crown Business.

Womack, J. P., Jones, D. T., & Roos, D. (2007). *The machine that changed the world.* Simon and Schuster.

Yow, V. R. (2014). *Recording oral history: A guide for the humanities and social sciences* (3rd ed.). Rowman & Littlefield.

Zetka, J. (1995). Union homogenization and the organizational foundations of plantwide militancy in the U.S. automobile industry, 1959-1979. *Social Forces,73*(3), 789–810. doi.org/10.1093/sf/73.3.789

Appendix D
Toyota Oral History-Style Questions

Previous role

What company did you work for prior to Toyota?

How would you summarize your overall management style at that time?

What was your and your organization's approach to problems?

Before Toyota

How did you first learn about Toyota Georgetown?

What was the recruitment and interviewing process like?

What made you decide to take the job with Toyota?

Time at Toyota

Can you describe your start at Toyota?

Can you sketch or show me an organization chart relative to your position?

Did your management style change, if so how?

What were your primary learnings?

Did you have any "ah-ha" moments in Japan or in Georgetown?

What was it like to start production at TMMK?

After Toyota

What was your next role change within or outside of Toyota?

How did you apply what you learned at the early days at Georgetown to your next job?

Looking back, would you have done anything differently?

Conclusion

Are there any stories you wish you would have shared with me that you didn't?

Is there any additional advice you would like to share with me or potential readers?

Is there anything you said you would like redacted? If there is, please contact me at anytime.

Appendix E
Sensei Characteristics

1. Demographics: Age of the sensei compared to you
   a. Same age
   b. Sensei was older
   c. Sensei was younger
   d. Don't remember

2. Demographics: Experience/knowledge
   a. Sensei had more knowledge/experience than me.
   b. Sensei had less knowledge/experience than me.
   c. Knowledge/experience didn't matter.

3. Duration of developmental relationship with sensei
   a. Short-term
   b. Long-term

4. Regularity of interactions
   a. Single interaction
   b. Regular schedule
   c. Unscheduled

5. Medium of interaction
   a. Face-to-face
   b. Distance
   c. Combination

6. Span of Interaction
   a. Dyadic, just the two of us
   b. Group-Oriented
   c. Multiple senseis

7. Organizational distance/direction: Direction
   a. Lateral (we were about the same on the organization chart)
   b. Downward (sensei was lower than me on the organization chart)
   c. Upward (sensei was higher than me on the organization chart)
   d. Different hierarchy

8. Location:
   a. Internal
   b. External

9. Purpose of Interaction.
   a. General development
   b. Specific development

10. Timeframe/purpose of interaction
    a. Short-term performance
    b. Long-term development

11. Degree of Structure: Formality
    a. Informal/unstructured
    b. Programmatic/formal

12. Development coordinator.
    a. Highly involved
    b. Available

13. Choice to participate
    a. Self-select/volunteer
    b. Mandatory

14. How did your relationship with your sensei(s) begin?
    a. Entirely chosen by me
    b. Negotiated upon initiation

c. Cooperative or mutual process
d. Sensei was assigned to me

15. What best describes the context of initiation with your sensei
    a. Hiring interview
    b. Formal interactions
    c. Directly reported to sensei
    d. Informal decision of sensei to seek me out

16. Participant matching would be best described as:
    a. Naturally/unmatched; matching naturally occurred
    b. Formally matched

17. Choose the best answer.
    a. Preparation was provided prior to my relationship with my sensei.
    b. Support provided throughout my relationship with my sensei.

18. The sensei exhibited the following learning behaviors (select all that apply):
    a. Collaborating
    b. Directing
    c. Goal-setting
    d. Helping on assignments
    e. Modeling
    f. Observing
    g. Problem solving
    h. Proving practical feedback
    i. Sharing information, teaching

19. The sensei exhibited the following emotional behaviors (select all that apply):
    a. Affirming

b. Aiding
c. Befriending
d. Calming
e. Confidence-building
f. Counseling, Encouraging
g. Supporting

20. Career progression related
    a. Advocating
    b. Introducing
    c. Socializing

21. Characteristics of negative experiences with sensei
    a. Mismatched values
    b. Mismatched personality
    c. Mismatched work styles
    d. Intentional exclusion
    e. Neglect
    f. Self-absorption
    g. Inappropriate delegation
    h. General abuse of power
    i. Credit taking;
    j. Sabotage
    k. Deceit
    l. Technical incompetence
    m. Interpersonal incompetence
    n. Bad attitude
    o. Personal problems

22. Words that best describe your sensei-employee relationship)
    a. Sponsorship
    b. Exposure
    c. Visibility
    d. Coaching
    e. Protection

f. Challenging assignments
   g. Role modeling
   h. Acceptance
   i. Confirmation
   j. Counseling
   k. Friendship

23. My sensei was trustworthy
    a. Strongly disagree
    b. Disagree
    c. Slightly disagree
    d. Slightly agree
    e. Agree
    f. Strongly agree

24. Toyota was trustworthy
    a. Strongly disagree
    b. Disagree
    c. Slightly disagree
    d. Slightly agree
    e. Agree
    f. Strongly agree

25. Separation: How were you separated from your sensei?
    a. I was hired by a different organization.
    b. I transferred within the same organization to a different business unit or geographical area.
    c. The relationship ended as planned.
    d. Other.

26. Later relationship with sensei can be described as:
    a. I continued the previous mentor/protégé relationship.
    b. The relationship changed to one of a colleague/friend/collaborator.
    c. I had no further relationship with my sensei.

27. Gender relationship.
    a. Was your sensei the same or a different gender?
    b. Do you know of any opposite gender relationships?
    If so, how do you believe this factored into the success or lack thereof of the relationship?

Turning Points for Cultivation

1. Meaningful interactions
    a. Can you describe the most meaningful/memorable interactions with your sensei?
    b. What interactions with your sensei lead you to these memorable/meaningful moments?

2. Framing problems:
    a. Describe your frame of reference for problems as it related to before Toyota, during Toyota, and now.
    b. Did your sensei shape that frame of reference? In what ways?
    c. What was the first improvement or problems solving activity you witnessed?
    d. What was your first improvement or problem solved?

3. Mutual benefit:
    a. Did your sensei benefit from the relationship? In what ways?
    b. Did Toyota benefit from the relationship with your sensei? In what ways?

4. Task-Centered to Transformational
    a. What types of tasks did your sensei initially have you do?

b. How did you feel about these tasks?
   c. Were these tasks transformational? If so, in what ways?
   d. At what point did the tasks change from transactional to transformational?

5. 5. The sensei perspective
   a. Were you ever a mentor at or after Toyota?
   b. What did you learn about mentoring TPS?
   c. What worked?
   d. What didn't work?

Appendix F
Semi-Structured Interview Questions Regarding Mentors

1. Identifying, contacting, and acquiring a mentor or mentors
   a. What was your mentor experience like for you?
   b. What were some challenges and opportunities?
   c. Please tell me the name of your mentor: _____ .
   d. How did you acquire your mentor at Toyota?
   e. Was the experience difficult or easy for you?
   f. How would you compare your experience to others? Why?

2. Expectations of the mentor-mentee relationship implementing or adapting TPS
   a. What makes for a "good" mentor-mentee relationship?
   b. What is the role/function of a Mentor?
      i. Where do they contribute most, or are most helpful, to you?
   c. What were your expectations going into a mentor-mentee relationship?
      i. In what ways have your expectations of having a mentor been satisfied?
      ii. Frustrated?
   d. What do you see as your responsibilities in the relationship?
      i. What do you bring to it to make it a positive experience?

3. Actual experience of mentor-mentee relationships.

    a. What did you discuss with your mentor?
    b. How often did you communicate?
    c. How would describe your relationship with your Mentor?
    d. How would you describe your overall experience?
    e. Were or are you friends with your mentor?
        i. What were your mentor's hobbies?
    f. Did you feel that your mentor was qualified for the role?

4. Pros and cons in your experience of mentor-mentee relationships.
    a. What do you perceive as the benefits to you of having a mentor?
    b. How does having a mentor contribute to/inhibit your overall experience?
    c. If your relationship with your mentor were not "comfortable," how would you go about ending it?

5. Perceived barriers or inhibitors to acquiring and experiencing a positive mentor-mentee relationship.
    a. What is the biggest problem you experienced in relating to your mentor?
    b. What is the biggest problem you experienced in spending time with your mentor?
    c. What role do you think "gender" plays in mentor-mentee relationships?
        i. What gender was your mentor? _____ .
    d. What role do you think "ethnicity/culture" plays in mentor-mentee relationships?
        i. What ethnic/cultural background did your Mentor have? _____ .
    e. What sort of awkwardness have you experi-

enced in your mentor-mentee relationship related to either gender or ethnicity/culture?
   f. Do you feel that these factors ought to "match"?

6. Suggested improvements to the current program/model.
   a. What would make the mentor-mentee program better? easier? more productive?